THE FINANCIAL SYSTEM LIMIT

THE
FINANCIAL SYSTEM LIMIT

BRITAIN'S REAL DEBT BURDEN

DAVID KAUDERS

Sparkling Books

British Library Cataloguing in Publication Data. A catalogue record for this book is available from the British Library.

4.2

Printed in the United Kingdom by Short Run Press, Exeter

ISBN: 9781907230790
E-book: 9781907230776

United States 9781907230769; Australia and selected other countries 9781907230783.

OVERVIEW

This book shows that all schemes that borrow from the future are thwarted by three related concepts:

- the true cost of debt to society;
- the central banking economic cycle; and
- the financial system limit.

The author challenges the existing academic and political consensus about how economies should be managed. Estimates show that one-fifth of all economic output is spent on paying interest: this is too high an overhead and should not be allowed to increase. The old arguments about sound money versus stimulus, as well as contemporary arguments that governments controlling their own currency can create as much credit as they wish, are fundamentally inappropriate to the deflationary world that we are moving towards.

Whether you are a concerned individual, an academic, politician, banker or even a policymaker, read about a different view of the current financial orthodoxies, one that will provoke serious debate and even action.

"Radical thinkers might have a point" was how the *Financial Times* described David Kauders' first book *The Greatest Crash: How contradictory policies are sinking the global economy.* This new book offers further original thought.

ABOUT THE AUTHOR

David Kauders FRSA was educated at Latymer Upper School, Jesus College, Cambridge and Cranfield School of Management. He is an investment manager and also contributes occasional articles to the UK financial press.

TABLE OF CONTENTS

TABLE OF CONTENTS

TABLE OF CONTENTS

LIST OF TABLES

FIGURES

BY THE SAME AUTHOR

The Greatest Crash: How contradictory policies are sinking the global economy

Understanding Brexit Options: What future for Britain?

Bear Markets: When finance turns upside down (forthcoming)

PUBLISHER'S NOTE

This book was written and almost ready for publication before coronavirus[1] arrived. The author has added a chapter to the original manuscript to discuss the interaction between the financial system limit and the economic shock following the pandemic.

Some of the data for this book was researched in 2018 and slightly more recent figures will be found by following the references given. The same 2018 data appears in a number of sources that are also referred to by this book. For consistency, the author has chosen not to update the figures, particularly in Chapter 2. The arguments presented are unaffected by the date at which debt statistics were collected.

PUBLISHER'S NOTE

The publisher would particularly like to thank:

- *thechartstore.com* for US Treasury Bill rates in Figure 1, the lower line on the cover, and for Figure 7;
- *wallethub.com* for US credit-card interest rates in Figure 1 and the upper line on the cover;
- Geordie Clarke and Lynn Curtis for their editorial advice;
- Karl Hunt for the design and Sharon Laverick for the index.

Copyright permission has been granted or requested where appropriate.

DEFINITIONS AND EXPLANATIONS

Throughout this book, the -$- symbol means US dollars. Dates on charts reproduced from US sources are in US format, i.e. month/day/year. The non-technical reader will also find the following definitions and explanations useful:

Positive nominal interest rates

The normal condition when depositors and bond holders earn interest on their investment, sometimes called 'yield.' Bank borrowers pay a higher rate than earned by depositors, whereas the cost of interest paid by bond issuers is the same as bond holders earn.

Negative nominal interest rates

For bank deposits, negative nominal interest rates occur when the bank charges the depositor a fee based on value for depositing money.

In bond markets, negative nominal interest rates occur when a bond is bought at a premium over redemption value and the premium exceeds the cumulative value of all interest coupons from purchase to maturity. These interest coupons are insufficient to offset the capital loss.

Lower bound to interest rates

When nominal interest rates are negative, this concept says "but interest rates cannot go *very* negative." The lower bound is, as yet, unknown.

Positive real interest rates

Interest paid by borrowers and/or received by depositors exceeds the rate of inflation. This is different from a past era when inflation exceeded either interest earned or the cost of borrowing and thus eroded its true value or cost.

Negative real interest rates

For depositors and bond buyers, interest received is less than the rate of inflation. For borrowers and bond issuers, interest paid is less than the rate of inflation. Negative real interest rates are therefore good for borrowers but bad for depositors.

Sound money

Sound money represents the constant value of goods and services in circulation, without any artificial attempt by the authorities to expand the money supply.

Administered rates

Rates under the direct control of central banks, usually the interest rate at which they will lend to commercial banks.

* * *

In recent years the deposit rate earned has been persistently below the inflation rate. However, borrowers have paid more than the inflation rate. Thus depositors have received negative real interest rates while at the same time borrowers have paid positive real interest rates.

Except in the case of inflation-linked bonds, interest rates earned on all types of bond purchases are fixed according to the price paid. Future inflation rates may well be different to current rates, and in a deflationary world they will be lower, possibly even negative. Hence prospective real interest rates matter, whether you are a depositor or a borrower. The true earnings (if any) from deposits and the true cost of borrowing will both be more if the general level of prices falls, that is, if inflation gives way to deflation, even if some prices rise.

"Practical men, who believe themselves to be quite exempt from any intellectual influences, are usually the slaves of some defunct economist. Madmen in authority, who hear voices in the air, are distilling their frenzy from some academic scribbler of a few years back."

— *John Maynard Keynes*

INTRODUCTION

This book argues that stimulating economies to escape recession is a short-term policy that brings longer-term problems not foreseen by policy-makers or the public. Far from maintaining comfortable living standards, the established practice of credit expansion, by various means, is causing slow economic decline and deepening the world's debt problems.

I first introduced the concept of the financial system limit in my book *The Greatest Crash: How contradictory policies are sinking the global economy*, published in 2011. The concept, which will be explored in Chapter 1, says that credit cannot be created *ad infinitum*. Then in 2013, in privately circulated material, I suggested that the global economy is now dictated by a new economic cycle created by central banks.

Although extensive economic statistics are published by governments and international bodies, I could find none that answered this question: **why are interest rates paid by borrowers significantly higher than interest rates offered to depositors?** I will explain how this scenario evolved and how positive real interest rates influence the financial system limit and the central banking economic cycle.

This book offers ideas for consideration, rather than an analytic exposition with spreadsheets and models. The discussion is in four parts:

1. Radical thoughts (Chapters 1 to 3), describing the financial bind the world faces.

2. Academic theory and case studies (Chapters 4 to 6).

3. Review of existing proposals and their limitations (Chapters 7 and 8).

4. Economic impact of the pandemic (Chapters 9 and 10), showing the depth of the debt problem.

There has been much debate between central bankers, particularly in Europe, about whether to continue with policies of stimulus or to adopt sound money in an attempt to cease inflating ailing economies. This book shows that both sides of the argument are wrong. Those promoting monetary and fiscal stimulus as a policy objective have slowly led the world into economic lethargy, from which there is no easy escape. Disciples of the opposing policy, sound money, have a point but it is not the cure for all the ills outlined in the three concepts at the core of this book.

The world was already drifting towards a global recession prior to the arrival of coronavirus. Nonetheless, every politician and official working to secure our financial future needs to understand the theories presented here. These concepts explain why economic growth was globally substandard and economies sluggish before the pandemic occurred. Superficially attractive financial remedies neither work in the long-term, nor help economic recovery.

David Kauders

(a founder member of Kauders Portfolio Management AG)

Zug, Switzerland, June 2021

PART ONE

THREE RADICAL THOUGHTS

1 THE FINANCIAL SYSTEM LIMIT

When someone borrows money to put food on the table, they are in financial difficulty. When they have no hope of even paying the mounting interest bill, let alone repaying their debt, they are bust. This can also happen to a country, when so many people are in financial difficulty that there is no hope of the indebted population honouring its debts even if some people within it are debt-free. In this situation the said country has reached its financial system limit. Neither action by the individual, nor policy change by the authorities, can work off the debt because too much is being spent on paying interest. The underlying problem will manifest itself in many ways: curtailed business activity; inability of consumers to keep spending; falling prices of assets that were propped up by easy credit; almost continual recession with only brief flashes of recovery. The financial system limit of any society is the debt level at which repayment ceases to be viable.

It is customary for economic statisticians to define highly indebted countries according to their government debt levels. However, for the purposes of this book, it is **total** debt that matters. Total debt is the sum of government debt, corporate plus banking system debt and personal debt. Personal debt itself consists of overdrafts, bank loans, mortgages and credit card debt.

Of the 36 current members of the Organisation for Economic Co-operation and Development (OECD), 28 feature in a list of countries having high levels of personal debt.[2] Personal debt is a developed-country problem. Prosperity has been bought, literally, on credit.

We have become used to central banks being able to conjure recoveries out of recessions. Each time a downturn has occurred, it has been swept away but downturns became deeper as the natural economic cycles of the past were augmented by policy-driven cycles. For example, in the United Kingdom, according to the Office for National Statistics, GDP fell by 4.2% in 2009, whereas in 1991 it only fell by 1.1%. In GDP terms, the dot com "bust" was represented by a lower growth rate.[3]

Serious financial and business journals have carried many reports and opinions about how central banks need to find new ways to counteract the recession caused by the global pandemic. The fashionable proposal is to use fiscal policy (that is, tax cuts and increased government expenditure) to stimulate economic activity. Such a policy can have no lasting benefit, for three reasons:

1. Stimulating economic activity needs increased credit, but banks will not lend to bad risks just because governments have changed accounting rules for bank capital and bad debts.

2. Tax cuts and/or increased government spending cause government deficits to rise. One could describe this as paying Peter now, to rob Paul in a few years time. This will lead the world into deflation.

3. New money raised by governments through borrowing will incur low positive real interest rates at the outset, but turn into high positive real interest rates when general price levels fall.

Over the past quarter of a century, rates paid to depositors have collapsed, yet rates paid by borrowers have stayed comparatively high. Figure 1 contrasts three-month US Treasury Bill rates (a proxy for interest paid to depositors) with the average cost of US credit card debt including financing charges:[4]

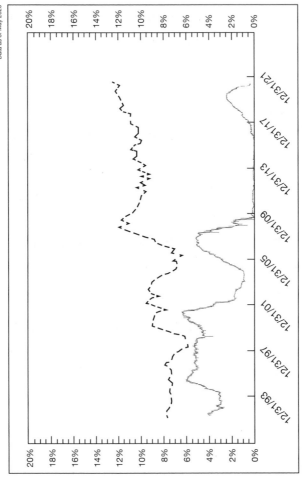

—— US Treasury bills, example of interest rates received   - - - US credit-card borrowing rates

Figure 1 Paying more to the banking system

Comparing paid and earned interest rates in this way reveals how expensive credit is. From 1993 to 2001, the difference between the two rates was around 9%. In 2003, in the wake of the dot com crash, deposit rates hit new lows, with Treasury Bills only paying 0.81%. But at the same time, credit-card borrowers were paying around 14.7% on average, so the difference had risen to 13.9%. The credit crunch subsequently drove Treasury Bills down to nil yield but a few months later credit card rates were climbing, with the difference, as at December 2019, at around 15.4%.

Debt repayment has a real cost because inflation is so low. When real interest rates are positive and rates paid by borrowers exceed the inflation rate, borrowing consumes financial resources. For example, when inflation is 1% and credit-card borrowing costs 13%, the real rate of interest is 12%. Prior to the era of monetary management by central banks, real interest rates were usually 2% to 3%.

Symptoms of debt problems caused by excessive interest costs vary by country. In many cases, they can be measured directly by statistics such as consumer loan defaults. In Britain, food bank use is an indirect measure of debt problems.

Following the 1987 stock market crash, the credit floodgates were opened wide to encourage more borrowing. When continuing that policy proved ineffective after the millennium boom and bust, quantitative easing was invented to push credit into the Japanese economy. This was later copied by other central banks although the methodology is now seen as ineffective. Instead of contriving ever more extreme measures to expand credit, why not ask what is preventing continued economic growth?

It is impossible for debt to expand to infinity because the cost of servicing it would then also be infinite. The financial system limit is determined by the cost of borrowing. It is best defined as **the proportion of economic output spent on interest on total debt, above which that debt can no longer be repaid in full.**

A LOGICAL PROOF

Existence of the financial system limit can be proved by logic:

1. Postulate that it does not exist and therefore debt can expand to infinity.

2. No matter how low interest rates charged to borrowers may go, any percentage of infinity is itself infinity. Therefore if debt can expand to infinity, interest paid must also expand to infinity.

3. Interest has to be defrayed from what is earned. Earnings can only be achieved by selling goods or services at a

price others can afford. Therefore paying infinite interest requires trading an infinite supply of goods and services.

4. But an infinite supply of goods and services for sale can only be achieved if resources of people and nature are themselves infinite.

5. Since the supply of raw materials is finite and an infinite population could not feed itself, the proposition that debt can expand to infinity cannot be true.

2 DEBT INTEREST IS A COST TO SOCIETY

The world is in a financial bind caused by the weight of existing debt. We need to look at the elements involved to try to understand what has happened. The factors that matter most are:

1. Total debt in the world.
2. Total assets in the world.
3. World economic output.

When I searched academic sources for 'World debt total,'[5] a report by Bloomberg dated 15 January 2019 stated this was $244 trillion at the third quarter of 2018. Since debt is a balance sheet figure, one has to assume this was the position as of 30 September 2018, although this was not made clear. The report broke down debt into four components:

Table 1 Sectoral debt at 3rd quarter 2018

Government	$65.2 trillion
Households	$46.1 trillion
Non-financial corporates	$72.9 trillion
Financial sector	$60.0 trillion

The accuracy and reliability of any set of statistics can always be queried, but these figures do seem to be a reasonable estimate. The same aggregate figure was quoted by the *Financial Times*[6] (further discussion in Chapter 10).

According to a recent report by Credit Suisse, world assets totalled $317 trillion at 'mid-2018.'[5]

What is the value of the world's economic output? A search for 'World GDP 2018' produced a tight range of figures from $78 trillion to $84.8 trillion, taken from estimates made by the World Bank, OECD, United Nations and others. Based on these, $80 trillion seemed a reasonable approximation (GDP, gross domestic product, is the usual measure of the size of any country's economy.)

In summary, key figures for the global economy are:

Table 2 World economy 2018, approximate data only

World debt	$244 trillion
World asset value	$317 trillion
Annual world economic output	$80 trillion

These figures tell us therefore that world debt is around three times the size of the world economy. Debt equals credit, which is the money we all spend. In the United Kingdom, notes and coins account for only 1.1% of money.

ESTIMATING THE COST OF INTEREST ON DEBT

All debt brings interest cost, which takes a substantial toll on economic prosperity. In order to estimate the total cost, it is necessary to make separate estimates for corporate, household and government debt interest costs. For this purpose, we will include financial sector debt within corporate debt.

The weighted average cost of debt of companies in Germany, Austria and Switzerland was reported by KPMG in 2018 to be 2.9% per annum.[7] This includes all forms of borrowing by companies, both in debt markets and from banks but excludes equity cost. Calculation of a weighted average does not cause any bias by size of company.

This data, however, relates to countries with very low interest rates. We need a global average cost of debt for businesses. The only guide I could find[8] reports US investment grade debt costing 6.8% and high-yield debt costing 8.17%. Interest rates reported for bank loans vary so widely that the data cannot be used. But compared to the 2.9% rate of low interest countries, US corporate borrowing rates of around

7% seem mid-range. Since the United States is hardly one of the more expensive countries for business borrowing, we will take 7% as a rough guide to the cost of interest for businesses.

Money borrowed by households (individuals and families), other than mortgages, costs more: even in these low-yield times, the charge for unsecured debt sold to the general public is well into double figures. A quick internet search in August 2019 produced advertisements with interest rates of 21.9% in the USA, and up to 49.9% in the United Kingdom. Headline rates themselves may be understated thanks to "special offers" that run out, forcing the borrower to pay much more after a few months.

Although interest paid *to* investors is very low or non-existent in many cases, that paid *by* personal borrowers remains high. In an extreme example, some United Kingdom banks now charge 39.9% for unapproved overdrafts and, in a few cases, even more.

Estimating the interest cost of household (personal) debt is less certain. Property is generally seen as a safe asset and therefore mortgage interest rates can be below some corporate borrowing rates. Mortgage rates, however, often vary over time, even where there are initial fixed rate periods. At the other extreme, credit card borrowing rates can be exorbitant (see above and Chapter 1). Therefore I have assumed an average cost of personal debt at 12% per annum, somewhere between the best mortgage rates and average credit card cost in 2018.[9] This is an assumption, not a proven figure, but the United Kingdom average rate of credit card interest paid was reported as 20.77% at March 2020.[10]

There is no single figure that can be easily found for the total interest cost of all government debt. There are statistics for selected countries giving government debt to GDP and government debt to government income ratios. Again it is necessary to adopt a median estimate. The market interest rate on government bonds for major countries varies between -0.59% for Switzerland and 7.31% for Brazil according to tradingeconomics.com.[11] The same site reported the following yields on government debt of major economies:

Table 3 Debt costs of selected major governments

Country	Debt term	Interest rate
Switzerland	10 years	-0.59%
Germany	10 years	-0.36%
United Kingdom	10 years	0.77%
United States	10 years	2.02%
China	30 years	3.94%
India	3 years	7.02%
Brazil	10 years	7.31%

At the other extreme, there are some countries whose governments pay borrowing rates in double figures. Examples at the same date included Venezuela (10.43%),

Kenya (11.75%), Nigeria (14.09%), Pakistan (14.1%), and Zambia (29.0%).

Many Western countries have government debt costing below 3% of amount borrowed and in some cases negative yields are on offer. But heavyweights such as Brazil and India pay over 7%. What is the global average cost for government debt of all countries therefore? In the absence of more precise figures, I will use an average government debt cost of 4%. Since government debt is only just over a quarter of total world debt, an approximation may not matter. Substituting 3% instead of 4% would reduce the global average cost of interest by only 0.27%.

Putting these three estimates together using the data in Table 1 gives an average cost of all debt types of 7.2% per annum, and therefore debt service for the world is around $17.5 trillion (7.2% of $244 trillion). It follows that approximately 21.9% of world economic output is spent on interest costs (i.e. $17.5 trillion as a proportion of $80 trillion). This has to be a drain on economies globally.

It is reasonable to conclude that around 21 - 22% of world economic output is spent on paying interest. To err slightly on the side of caution, this book will suggest one-fifth, which may well be an understatement. Because we are using estimates, I will also round the cost of interest down to $17 trillion. Figure 2 explains this relationship. Seven percent of debt seems reasonable, until one realises that 7% of debt,

$17 trillion out of $244 trillion, is a higher **proportion** of economic output. The cost of debt service has to be defrayed from the smaller value of economic output:

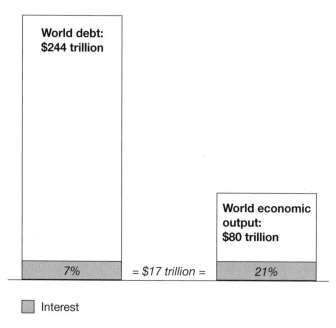

Figure 2 Interest matters

EXAMPLES OF THE SCALE OF DEBT

How debt is acquired and used can vary between countries. The underlying mechanism is the bank credit multiplier. Deposit a pound, dollar or Euro in a bank and the bank lends it out more than once. This is called fractional reserve banking. These steps show how credit multiplies:

1. Using money deposited with it, Bank A creates a loan account for a borrower.

2. The borrower spends the money.

3. Each time the borrower spends some of the money, it stays in the banking system. It may go back to Bank A if the supplier also banks with Bank A. Or it may go to another bank, Bank B.

4. Money received in this way is treated as a new deposit, and therefore it is lent out again, even though the original loan made by Bank A is outstanding.

5. All banks in the same banking system exchange net payments daily through their central bank, keeping the expanding supply of loans within each countries' banking system.

As an example of debt creation through this credit multiplier, consider Britain. Until about forty-five years ago, United Kingdom regulations prevented banks creating more than £3 Sterling for every pound deposited with them. Then the regulations were relaxed and six times became the norm, enabling credit to expand more rapidly, as these more recent figures show:

Table 4 UK debt 1996 vs. 2017

	1996	*2017*
Government debt	44% of GDP	88% of GDP
All other debt (household and corporate incl. financial sector)	153% of GDP	230% of GDP
Total debt	197% of GDP	318% of GDP

At the start of this recent twenty-one-year period, total debt was less than twice the size of the United Kingdom's economy. By 2017, it had risen to over three times the size of the 2017 economy, (which was itself larger than in 1996). Since this relationship is the same as between world debt and world economic output, it follows that approximately one-fifth of British economic output (GDP) is now spent on interest.

Now consider some of the specific debt problems in Britain. The Bank of England has warned about risks in the high level of personal debt. But they created this through quantitative easing! Most of the rise in the percentage of debt to size of the economy has followed from the credit injections designed to aid recovery from the dot com crash and then the 2008 credit crunch. Student debt is another sore subject: in 1996, it was negligible. By 2017 it had risen to about 5% of GDP following a change in government policy whereby student loans replaced state grants financed from taxes.

The United Kingdom does have a growing problem with falling living standards. Its rate of population growth is steady at around 0.6% per annum, thanks to a much higher rate of births over deaths. Taking calendar 2019 compared to the previous year, the Office for National Statistics (ONS) reported that the British economy (GDP) grew by 3.3% at market prices.[12] The United Kingdom uses two different inflation measures, Consumer Price Index (CPI), and Retail Price Index (RPI). CPI omits some incidental housing costs and shows lower values than RPI, particularly when mortgage interest rates rise. For 2019 as a whole, the ONS reported CPI of 1.8% and RPI of 2.7%.

The standard of living that matters to people is their personal income and how it has changed. To measure this, we need to calculate GDP *per capita* in inflation-adjusted terms. Using the RPI figure for inflation, 3.3% economic growth is identical to RPI 2.7% plus population growth of 0.6%. This means that *per capita* living standards in 2019 were unchanged from 2018. Using the lower CPI inflation rate of 1.8%, per capita living standards in 2019 were only up by 0.9% over 2018 (i.e. 3.3% - 0.6% - 1.8%).[13]

Apart from the political choice made by ignoring adjustments for inflation and population change, this data tells us that the United Kingdom economy was struggling in 2019. Perhaps debt servicing cost may have been a factor. The United Kingdom is not an extreme case with very high debts: its debt is average for the world and therefore the United Kingdom is a good model to use. Since the United Kingdom is average, global debt may also have grown faster than world economic output.

What about other countries? The United States has average debt characteristics, with ratios of private debt to GDP and government debt to GDP broadly similar to the United Kingdom. In Japan the non-government debt to GDP ratio is 231%, similar to both the United Kingdom and United States. However, Japanese government debt is about 250% of GDP. Taken together, the figures indicate that Japan has a somewhat more serious debt problem than the United Kingdom or United States.

Some commentators dismiss concerns about Japanese debt on the grounds that most government debt is held within Japan, so that external debt is relatively low. 14% of Japanese Government Bonds are held outside Japan, whereas 28% of UK Gilts and 29% of US Treasury Bonds are held outside the United Kingdom and United States respectively.[14]

This argument is incorrect. The interest cost of all debt is a cost to society: Japanese people are paying interest at a level that prevents economic progress, causing every attempt at economic stimulus to fizzle out after a few years. With total debt approaching five times GDP, Japan is stuck in a debt trap, its own financial system limit. Parcelling up the problem into internal and external debt, or government and private debt, obscures the total cost of all debt.

WHERE DOES ALL THE INTEREST GO?

The world spends about one-fifth of its economic output on interest. What does the financial sector do with the interest it earns? Here we must distinguish interest paid to banks and interest paid by both governments and businesses raising money through bond sales. Interest paid by governments on their debt and interest paid by companies on their corporate bonds goes directly to investors. Low yield government debt is a safe asset, whereas high yield corporate debt is risky. Prudent investors in high yield debt should treat a portion of that interest as compensation against risk of loss of capital in event of a default.

All interest paid by the household sector and a substantial proportion of interest paid by the corporate sector, is paid directly to banks and other financial sector lending businesses.

Since the credit crunch, bankers have been under political pressure not to overpay themselves. Yet the widening gap in interest rates paid *by* borrowers and paid *to* depositors must have an explanation. There are three possible causes:

1. One is that loan losses have risen: all borrowers must pay for defaults.

2. Banks have been squeezed financially by falling interest rates.

3. The third is that bank overheads have risen.

Let's look at loan losses first. Here are some recent loan loss rates as a percentage of all bank loans, by country, in 2017:

Table 5 Loan losses of all banks in selected countries in 2017[15]

Country	Losses %
United Kingdom	0.7
United States	1.1
Italy	14.4
Japan	No data

There are two distinct pictures here, countries with low loan losses and those who are exceptions.

The United States and United Kingdom are typical and similar economies in their debt ratios. The general picture in these economies is that loan losses are under control. Banks know who to lend to and who to avoid. Therefore high consumer borrowing rates do not stem directly from default rates.

For specific reasons in each case, Italy and Japan are exceptions. Italy had some serious debt losses in 2017, following the failures of Banca Monte dei Paschi di Siena, Banca Popolare di Vicenza and Veneto Banca, so the data may not be normal annual statistics for Italy. Japan has unusual accounting standards that allow postponement of repayments when borrowers are in difficulty, rather than writing the loans off. It is impossible to measure bad debts in Japan.

The squeeze on the financial structure of banks arises from net interest margins being reduced. The extreme example of this occurs in countries whose central banks charge commercial banks for the privilege of depositing money with them. Bank earnings depend on a surplus of borrowers paying more than each bank pays its depositors. This surplus has been in decline as the general level of interest rates has fallen. In consequence, banks seek to earn more from their lending businesses.

What about bank overheads? According to *The Economist,* Citigroup employed 30,000 people in compliance, risk and other control functions at end 2018, 15% of all employees, whereas ten years earlier, only 4% of its employees worked in compliance.[16] The same report noted that British banks spend £5 billion annually on anti-money laundering compliance; HSBC alone employs 5,000 people in this area.

This evidence shows that compliance has become a growth industry. In my view the rising difference between interest paid *to* depositors and interest paid *by* borrowers is partly related to the growth of compliance overheads. As deposit rates have fallen banks have avoided cutting lending rates in line with the trend, creating the margin that we saw in Figure 1 (Chapter 1) to pay for these increasing overheads. The cost of debt interest paid to banks in relation to the world's economic output therefore represents the overheads that have been accumulated to satisfy society's desire to control its banks.

3 THE CENTRAL BANKING ECONOMIC CYCLE

If you are involved in any type of business, you will be aware that business cycles are a fact of life. However, the nature of the economic cycle has changed. This chapter explains the radical change that has occurred.

TRADITIONAL ECONOMIC CYCLES

The simplest form of economic cycle can be found in agriculture: the pig cycle. This is how it works:

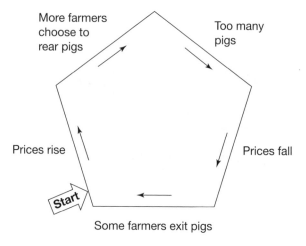

Figure 3 The pig cycle

Pigs need little land and feed off waste. When prices rise, more farmers choose to rear pigs and the supply of pork expands. Too many pigs are bred, prices fall and some farmers exit the business. Once supply falls too low, prices start to rise again...

Sows can produce two litters a year, and the time from conception to slaughter is about 310 days. Just two circuits of this cycle can take the whole market from shortage to oversupply.

The traditional business cycle taught to economics students is driven by expansion and contraction of inventory:

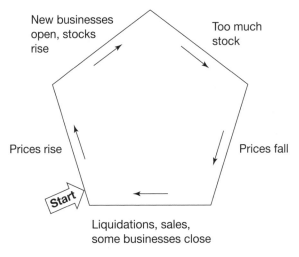

Figure 4 The inventory cycle

Both manufacturers and retailers carry inventory (stock of goods for sale). Inventory grows both in response to rising prices and because new businesses enter the market. When there is too much inventory, prices fall as surplus supply is offered to the market, then liquidation sales follow with some businesses closing. The cycle usually lasts four to seven years, then restarts.

THE SERVICE INDUSTRY CAPACITY CYCLE

During the second half of the twentieth century, the concept of the 'managed economy' appeared. In parallel with this, service businesses expanded. In many countries services are now the dominant economic activity. In an economy governed by services rather than manufacturing, a different cycle emerges. Whereas the pig and inventory cycles are similar in that physical assets increase or decrease, this cycle is driven by expansion and contraction of capacity to deliver services:

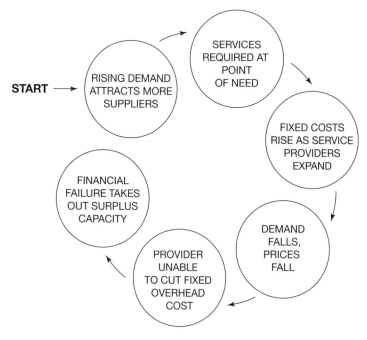

Figure 5 Service industry capacity cycle

Rising demand brings more suppliers into the market and causes existing suppliers to expand in order to satisfy the requirement for instant provision that is the essence of many services. New premises are acquired on lease, new computers bought to be written off over perhaps four or five years, and new staff hired. More businesses enter the market, then demand slips and there is not enough business to justify all those fixed overheads. The quickest way to cut costs is to sack staff, but lease and computer costs remain. Businesses then compete by cutting prices, trying to attract marginal work. When the majority do so, nobody earns enough to cover overheads. Think of past glorious names such as Thomas Cook, FlyBMI and Mothercare. As businesses liquidate, the market shrinks and eventually a new cycle can start again.

Brexit is demonstrating how the service industry capacity cycle works in practice. Since the European single market was created, Britain has excelled at providing cross-border services to 30 other countries. Although the City of London is the prime exhibit, many other professions have been selling services from the United Kingdom. Britain has built its economic house on sales of financial, legal, accountancy, manufacturing support, transport and even artistic services. Services are an all-or-nothing business but Brexit will create the need for service providers selling to the single market to relocate in order to remain in business. Those selling services only within the United Kingdom may survive, but those selling cross-border and staying based in the United Kingdom will face barriers to trade. Some will close.

All three cycles, the pig cycle, inventory cycle and the service industry capacity cycle, follow the same conceptual path, i.e. expansion and contraction of either physical assets or capacity to deliver services. They only vary in their specific industry details.

ANOTHER CHANGE STARTED WITH THE 1987 CRASH

Ever since the 1987 crash, the authorities have pushed credit out in attempts to neuter every downturn. Each time, their actions caused a recovery and prevented an immediate economic depression. But economies became lethargic, with both inflation and interest rates paid to depositors plummeting to unheard of low levels.

The result has been to create a new kind of economic cycle, illustrated in Figure 6. This artificial cycle created by the authorities is in *addition* to traditional economic cycles. I will call it the central banking economic cycle, but government finance departments are also involved in this mechanism:

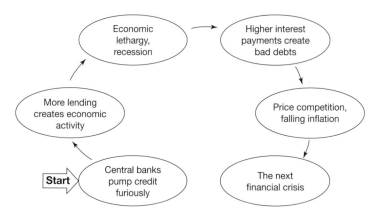

Figure 6 The central banking economic cycle

The authorities react to each economic crisis by expanding credit. Governments borrow to spend. Banks lend more to businesses and households. The first effect of this credit is to create more economic activity, leading to recovery but in time, the cumulative cost of debt interest starts to take effect, leading to economic lethargy and a new downturn. Higher interest payments themselves result in bad debts. Meanwhile the lack of economic activity causes price competition to break out between businesses. Lower prices are then reflected in lower inflation.

One of the side-effects of this cycle is discrimination between borrowers. Governments that are key to the global financial system can borrow cheaply, while others pay much more (see Chapter 2). Banks discriminate between borrowers, charging less to perceived good risks and more

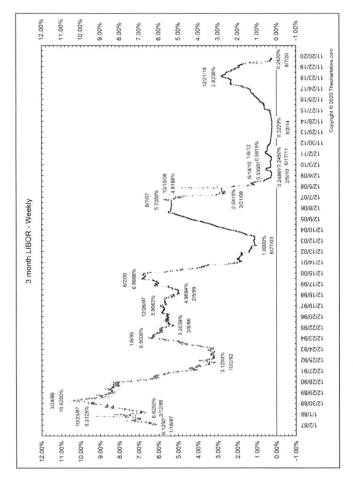

Figure 7 The long fall in London Inter-Bank Offered Rate (LIBOR) at 21st August 2020

to others. Standard overdraft rates no longer exist. Both real and nominal interest rates fall for good quality new borrowers, but those paying fixed rates find their true cost rising as prices and inflation decline. All these trends combine to lay the ground for the next financial crisis.

Policy-makers have therefore added a new dimension to the earlier economic cycles, forcing credit expansion by use of monetary tools upon the world, adding to the burdens faced by businesses and households.

The chart of weekly London Inter-Bank Offered Rate (LIBOR, a key interest rate) for 3-month borrowing (Figure 7) shows the pattern of decreasing recoveries following each recession.

The world is now starting the sixth iteration of the central banking economic cycle:

1. The first of these cycles was the Japanese boom in the late 1980s and subsequent bust, overlapping with the Western escape from the 1987 crash.

2. The second was the Asian boom, followed by the 1997 bust.

3. The third was the millennium boom and dot com bust.

4. The fourth was the 2002 to 2007 boom followed by the credit crunch.

5. Quantitative easing was used to drive recovery from the credit crunch, but this led to economic stagnation.

6. The authorities are now using both quantitative easing and fiscal stimulus in an attempt to neuter the economic effects of the pandemic and start another economic recovery.

Economic cycles always come to an end. The central banking economic cycle will be no exception.

PART TWO

ACADEMIC THEORY AND CASE STUDIES

4 ACADEMIC THEORY

Academics have extensively studied stock markets and capital formation. Surprisingly to me, the three key concepts highlighted by this book, namely the financial system limit, the interest cost of debt and the central banking economic cycle, do not feature in scholarly research. I searched for those three phrases without success. There was a reference to Minsky's theory of economic instability but nothing about debt limits caused by the cost of interest.

Two other academic theories have been much discussed in the past decade.

MODERN MONETARY THEORY

Modern Monetary Theory originated in American academic circles and is also popular with some American and British politicians, but mainstream economists do not accept it. The essence is that countries that issue their own currencies never have to repay their government debt. They can therefore issue as much new currency as they wish in order to stimulate economies, because they can issue new debt to replace maturing debt, or to pay the interest, or for them to spend.

The theory also argues that government provides the currency by which people trade and pay their taxes. Therefore the economy can be expanded by pumping more money into it as in the cases of the United States and United Kingdom.

Modern Monetary Theory aligns with the earlier 'quantity of money' theory and opposes the idea that higher interest rates fight inflation. It encourages governments to create an unlimited supply of money but doing this would result in an even faster rise in the debt burden and hence the total cost of interest. Yet the theorists claim that debt can expand without limit[17] and this is where the argument fails. Existing central bank policies such as quantitative easing and outright monetary transactions already increase the debt burden. This book has shown there is no benefit in increasing it even faster. Modern Monetary Theory also claims that the natural rate of interest is zero, whereas permanently zero rates are specific to Islamic banking.

This theory is therefore inconsistent with the problem of unaffordable debt. It ignores the wastefulness of a fifth of global economic output channelled into paying interest. It says nothing about the central banking economic cycle.

Of course, these objections also apply to conventional economic analysis. Stimulating economies with more credit comes up against the same barriers.

CAPITAL AND NATIONAL INCOME THEORY

A few years ago, a book by Thomas Piketty, an economics professor in Paris, caught popular attention.[18] Piketty carried out extensive research into capital values, income flows and the economic connections between them.

In this author's view, the relationship between capital growth and economic activity ought to allow for the effects of deliberate monetary policies. Some of this monetary expansion flowed into asset prices, notably shares and property, but Piketty did not mention the equal and opposite debt created by such policies. This seems to be an omission from the scope of his work. But notice that Piketty limited himself to *government* debt, omitting household and corporate debt. His index entry for debt reads: 'Debt, see Public debt.'

Piketty proposed that the ratio of capital value to flow of income is equal to the savings rate divided by the growth rate. In numbers, a savings rate of 12% and a growth rate of 2% will yield a capital stock to flow of income ratio of 6. However, there is no mention of what happens when one of the numbers in this ratio turns negative. In recessions, the growth rate is negative and therefore capital ought to shrink. And in some types of expansion, for example the one in Britain prior to the credit crunch, high borrowing by consumers and businesses was a characteristic. Such expansions feature a negative savings rate. How can a negative divided by a positive, or a positive divided by a negative, define the capital to income ratio? In my view, this ratio should either be positive, or capital ought to be redefined by *deducting* debt to obtain a net figure.

Piketty's central thesis states that when the return on capital exceeds the growth rate in the economy, the rich get richer. The neo-liberal economic policies of recent years have given emphasis to market freedoms and removal of regulation at the expense of any broad interest of society.

Nonetheless, Piketty argued that the world needed and could afford new taxes on wealth. He proposed that capital owned by the population should be taxed and the proceeds used to pay down government debt. However, this could only work on a small scale, because of the unfortunate fact that selling assets to pay taxes depresses asset prices, which in turn reduces the value of further sales. Taxing assets works the first time, but its effect reduces the benefit to society of further such taxation. The small number of countries which tax wealth annually apply percentage rates typically below 1%, probably for this reason.

Apart from noting Britain's high debt levels, Piketty said nothing about the huge growth in the credit supply and consequent rise in total debt.

THE TOPICAL DEBATE

In 2019 there was a lively debate in the press about the limitations of economic theory. People were trying to find explanations for the odd economic behaviour but could not. *The Economist*[19] drew attention to the world economy's strange new rules, based on the failure of monetary policy to create inflation. A few days later, the *Financial Times* warned about economic policy failures[20] then published a letter[21] about negative interest rates in Sweden leading first to boom, then to bust.

At the same time, another older debate reappeared: sound money versus stimulus. As a consequence of the hyperinflation that struck Germany in 1923, with its terrible social and then political consequences, German economists have a deep commitment to sound money. The German constitution limits monetary expansion. However, the European Central Bank has been following policies of stimulus similar to other central banks, raising concerns among German economists and others.

On 4 October 2019, six former leading European central bankers published a memo outlining their concerns.[22] To simplify the technical arguments, they said that the European Central Bank was:

- failing to achieve its inflation target;
- threatening price stability;
- creating asset bubbles;
- depriving people of savings opportunities;
- using monetary tools to finance governments (which is prohibited by European treaties);
- creating negative side-effects in the banking, insurance and pension systems; and
- keeping weak businesses afloat.

A leading article in the *Financial Times* on 7 October 2019[22] commented on these arguments, describing the authors as 'dinosaurs.'

This dispute has been rumbling in academic and banking circles for some years. It is sometimes described as 'hawks' versus 'doves.' Reality is more complex. Some countries run surpluses, notably tax havens such as the Cayman Islands, financial centres such as Switzerland and Hong

Kong, and countries in which savings predominate such as Germany. Others run deficits, which have to be funded by borrowing. Deficits are particularly common in less-developed countries which often depend on international aid or remittances from citizens working abroad to balance their books. The biggest deficit country is the United States, but as it is the lynchpin of the global financial system, it can readily fund its deficits.

The concepts outlined in this book show that sound money versus stimulus is the wrong debate; and also that Modern Monetary Theory does nothing to solve the global cost of interest. What is needed is to:

- reduce the cost of interest, rather than add to it;
- recognise that debt cannot expand to infinity;
- recognise that spending one-fifth of global economic output on interest has brought the world close to the limits of the present financial system; and
- admit that official central banking policies are driving a new economic cycle, in which overall economic lethargy increases.

INFLATION TARGETS CAUSE DEFLATION

Throughout the neo-liberal years, inflation targets have been a key factor in economic policy. Instead of governments setting inflation rates, power was handed to central banks to pursue market-friendly policies. A modest amount of inflation is perceived as desirable, since the alternative, deflation, would herald prolonged economic contraction.

Inflation targets set by politicians encourage central banks to create credit, driving the world closer to the financial system limit. The extra real burden of interest payments then makes the postponed deflation more severe. Deflation usually involves falling asset prices, reduced incomes, debt defaults and public misery. This may be painful but cannot be fought with more stimulus. **In my view, the cost of interest is now depressing economic prosperity.** Deflation reduces governments' ability to raise taxes, since 'fiscal drag' reverses. Wherever tiered tax rates are in effect, deflation brings people into a *lower* tax bracket. As a result, the economic squeeze slowly tightens and as taxation revenues fall, public services deteriorate further.

Superficially, purchasing power rises as prices fall, but there is no such thing as 'good' deflation heralding economic benefits. Falling prices result in losses somewhere: job losses as businesses cancel investment plans; reduced pensions as falling investment values and lower dividends hit fund values. Debts become harder to service and repay. Economic relationships turn upside down; the global economy goes into reverse with deflation the driving force. Reduced incomes lead to less purchasing power, negating the superficial argument that people have more to spend. These dynamics add to the overhead burden of the cost of interest on existing debt, since the same interest has to be defrayed out of reduced incomes. Adjusted for deflation, low nominal interest rates then become high real interest rates, adding to the repayment burden.

Cutting deposit interest rates to zero has produced little economic benefit. The policy has discouraged saving, instead encouraging excessive consumer spending and investment in riskier assets. In some countries, negative deposit interest rates have taken the place of lower rates. As an example, the Swiss central bank charges commercial banks to deposit Swiss francs. Governments such as Germany have been able to sell bonds with a loss on their total return to redemption, because investors cherish return *of* principal more than return *on* principal. Such low interest rates have benefited Western governments by keeping their debt service costs down. The public and businesses have missed out.

In the inflationary years from the 1960s to the early 1980s, inflation eroded debt away. It made great sense to be a borrower and no sense at all to have a fixed income. Real interest rates were negative. This period was an aberration, not the norm. Inflation has now disappeared in most advanced economies, although it is still significant in some others such as parts of Latin America. Nonetheless, economists defined a misery index as the sum of the rates of inflation and unemployment. Ten percent inflation plus twenty percent unemployment gave a misery index value of 30. Fifteen percent inflation plus ten percent unemployment gave a misery index of only 25.

For advanced economies with negligible inflation, perhaps the misery index should be redefined. The inflation rate should be replaced by the average cost of consumer borrowing, giving a feel for how contemporary deflationary financial conditions affect the average household. For many, misery is now the cost of debt interest plus the unemployment rate, not the former basis of the inflation and unemployment rates added together. Perhaps in the inflation-prone countries it will be the sum of all three rates.

Since the global economy moved into positive real interest rates around 1982, borrowing has swung from being a blessing to a curse. Before the adoption of Keynesian stimulus, the historical norm was for borrowing to cost real money – that is, for interest rates *paid* to exceed the rate of inflation, resulting in rising real costs of borrowing. These times have returned. Cheap government borrowing today will turn out to be expensive as deflation takes hold. Instead of making a static comparison of current options, proposals for raising public finance should take account of the probable dynamics of change. For nearly four decades, disinflation has been a driving force in the global economy. Disinflation is likely to turn into outright deflation if debts created by deliberate monetary policy overwhelm the world.

Now that average interest rates paid exceed the inflation rate, there is no economic multiplier that can create more economic growth above the extra cost of interest on artificially created credit. The efforts of central banks to target inflation by creating artificial money so as to promote growth have had the opposite effect, with growing numbers of highly indebted businesses, households and countries forming a natural brake on economic activity.

Inflation targets no longer work. In my view, the unstated policy to 'inflate existing debts away' is failing. Instead of debating how to create more inflation, or how much stimulus is needed to prolong artificial economic growth, policy-makers need to consider how to *escape* this brake on economic activity caused by excessive debt.

5 TWO CASE STUDIES OF THE FINANCIAL SYSTEM LIMIT

The two case studies that follow are very different. They show that the interest cost of debt can manifest in strange ways. The first example should be familiar to American readers and the second to British ones.

PUERTO RICO

Puerto Rico was a Spanish territory until 1898, when it was ceded to the United States. It has an unusual constitutional position, as it is not a full State, rather being described as a 'Commonwealth.' There is a long history of unfunded budgets being balanced by more borrowing. Eventually this led to bankruptcy under a law crafted for that purpose during the presidency of Barack Obama.

In Puerto Rico, government debt ballooned. Under pressure from widespread poverty, excessive public debt and hurricane damage, it reached $74 billion by 2017, whereas fifteen years earlier it was around $30 billion. Unfunded pension liabilities account for a further $49 billion, making $123 billion in all.

This debt is scheduled for repayment over thirty years, which is an average principal repayment of $4.1 billion annually. Yet service cost for interest plus scheduled principal repayments is estimated at $43 billion per annum[23] for the same thirty-year period. Therefore interest is averaging about $38.9 billion *annually*.

The GDP of Puerto Rico is about $103 billion and shrinking slowly. Declining living standards led to an outward flow of workers, exacerbating the economic pressure. High costs of imports and energy also contributed.[24] The cost of interest, around 38% of GDP, is far too high for an economy under serious pressure.

There were other factors that pushed Puerto Rico along the path to insolvency. As debt matured it was replaced at *higher* interest rates. A tax concession whereby American companies were able to invest in Puerto Rico and receive income tax-free was withdrawn, setting the economy back further. State utilities such as water, sewerage, electricity and transport made losses year after year, funded by additional borrowing. Creditors have alleged there is inefficient revenue collection, with overpaid public employees. They proposed that Puerto Rico should seek to grow its way out of financial difficulty. This is impossible.

Three separate groups have lost money. The first group were those who sold their holdings of Puerto Rican debt several years ago because secondary capital market prices were falling. Whether their losses were more or less than the other two groups who held on is unknown.

The second group were creditors in the bankruptcy. Various hedge funds acquired the debt at distressed prices in the bond market, hoping for a profit once a settlement was reached. They have been offered 64 cents on the dollar for bonds issued before 2012, 45 cents on the dollar for bonds issued in 2012 and 35 cents on the dollar for bonds issued in 2014. The alternative was for these creditors to file court actions and a list of the main hedge funds who chose this option, compiled from court filings, is accessible on the internet.[25]

The third group were also creditors in the bankruptcy, consisting of funds investing in municipal bonds. In the United States, it is normal for a municipality (local government) or State to issue debt with tax-free interest paid to its own residents. Puerto Rican debt is completely tax-free to American investors wherever they live. As a result, it appeared to be an attractive investment for municipal bond funds.

Although the Commonwealth also has a personal debt problem, we have only examined government debt. Puerto Rico defaulted because it reached its own financial system limit.

Unfortunately Puerto Rico is not an exceptional case. According to the Jubilee Debt Campaign,[26] the fifteen less-developed countries spending over 18% of government revenue on interest payments had average cuts in public spending of 13% between 2015 and 2018. This research only looked at the link between interest cost of government debt and government revenue, which as we have seen is itself only a small part of the total debt problem. However, it supports the case that there is a financial system limit and that it may vary by country.

CARILLION

The British engineering and contract maintenance company Carillion plc and five subsidiaries were put into compulsory liquidation on 15 January 2018. The business was laden with debt, some of it hidden from immediate view. The cost of debt service, unprofitable business (margins were too low), a decline in the number and value of new contracts and deficits in its pension funds, all combined to bring Carillion down.

Tracing the full extent of the liquidation is difficult. There were about 350 companies in the group, including 36 joint ventures that were not consolidated in the accounts as the parent company was only a minority shareholder. Most of the figures that follow relate to the parent company, with the exception of the construction company which was also liquidated. Both inter-company loans and joint debt guarantees by more than one company confuse understanding the overall loss.

Carillion's financial position had been deteriorating. When it went bust, the *Financial Times* reported its deficit as £2.119 billion not counting its pension deficit.[27] The accounts as at 31 December 2016, just over a year earlier, had reported the corresponding figure as £1.61 billion. Evidently the company had borrowed another £509 million in the intervening period.

The pension deficit reported in the 2016 accounts was £587 million. UK accounting treats this as a debt owed by the sponsoring company. However, pension deficits are a much wider problem than this single case study might indicate, and will be covered in the next chapter.

Apart from the human tragedy of lost jobs, the immediate effect of the failure was to put pressure on both many other businesses that supplied Carillion and the United Kingdom public sector. Two major United Kingdom hospital projects had to be offered to other contractors at higher prices, with delays to completion. The full economic impact may take several years to emerge.

What about the people who lent that £2.1 billion? The parent company had three main sources of funds: banks, trade creditors and sales of its debt in bond markets.

Bank losses were reported in the *Financial Times* as £1.3 billion. This appears to have been in a mixture of revolving credit, emergency loans, private placements of bonds and financing of the UK early payment facility, borrowed from the five largest UK banks. Carillion also issued convertible bonds direct to major international banks. According to *Financial News*[28] these were bought not by the banks themselves but by investment funds managed by these banks.

Before failing, Carillion encouraged its suppliers to use the 30 day early payment facility – costs paid by the supplier, not by Carillion. The British government had set up a supply chain finance system whereby suppliers could borrow 100% of their invoice value from banks. Carillion had lengthened its payment terms from 60 days to 120 days, so the only way suppliers could get paid earlier was to borrow against their own invoices, interest paid by the supplier. Not quite what the government had intended when introducing its "prompt payment code."

The liquidators of Carillion Construction estimated its own liabilities as £6.9 billion.[29] Trade creditor losses may have been more than originally thought.

The third source of funds were raised in the German private corporate debt market (Schuldschein loans). These loans are unlisted transferable certificates of debt obligations. Raising money using unlisted securities means there is no proper market and no disclosure regulation. Carillion was scraping the barrel for sources of funds. Companies under financial pressure have to pay higher interest rates on their debt and the temptation is for investors to buy the higher-interest income without always understanding the risk it represents. Such investors lose both capital and income when the business fails. Notice the similarity of losses in convertible bonds and Schuldschein loans with losses in municipal bond funds and Puerto Rican government debt?

The consequential losses caused by a failure such as Carillion have serious effects on society. Here are two examples:

- Workers who lose their jobs will not be able to afford their rent or mortgage repayments, leading to increased demand for public housing: forced sales and lower house prices, evictions for non-payment of rent.
- Former Carillion employees whose pensions were "defined benefit" (which is discussed in the next chapter)

face enforced losses. Those not yet at retirement age when Carillion collapsed get 90% of the first £38,505 annual pension, i.e. a maximum of £34,655. Those who had reached retirement age apparently get their pensions but future increases may be restricted or cancelled altogether.

The huge wave breaking on the shoreline may eventually recede, but those caught in the onslaught need rescuing by compassionate policy-makers.

6 PENSIONS

The Carillion case study in the previous chapter demonstrated the breadth of the problems caused by failure of an over-borrowed company. One of the consequences is the way occupational pensions are affected.

It is important to distinguish occupational pensions from state benefits. In the United Kingdom, state pensions are "pay as you go." The worker pays contributions which generate an entitlement, but the cash contributed is used to pay those drawing pensions at the time. Each worker's future pension therefore depends on tomorrow's workers paying taxes.

In contrast, occupational pensions build up investment funds to provide for retirement. Every country makes rules for what is allowed and not allowed by way of contributions paid and pensions taken.

These pensions fall into two types, defined benefit (where the annual amount of pension is specified) and defined contribution (where only contribution rates are set).

Defined benefit schemes were common in the past. The pension any worker could expect to receive in retirement was fixed and guaranteed by the employer. The problems with such schemes lie in their employer guarantees, which bring the sponsoring company or organisation exposure to investment risk and sometimes risk in the assumptions used to estimate future returns. When markets lose value as financial problems grow, these schemes could well assume zero or even negative returns in the future, rather than the more optimistic assumptions of the past. This matters in countries that allow pension funds to determine their solvency based on assumed future growth of their investments.

The ability of any defined benefit scheme to pay its guaranteed pensions rests on both the value of the scheme investments and its future pension commitments. To factor both into any assessment of pension viability, the future liabilities to pay pensions are discounted to present values. "Discounting" means the current cost of each future year's pension is calculated making an assumption about the interest to be earned from now until that future year. As interest rates fall, the present value of these future liabilities rises. A scheme is solvent if its investments (assets) exceed its liabilities (present value of future pensions).

Defined contribution schemes pass all investment risk to the worker, who has a fund that is either used to buy an annuity or may be drawn on directly to pay a pension, but no employer guarantee as to the amount of future pension. In theory the worker takes his or her own investment decisions. In practice, the individual may take recommendations from an insurance company representative or other financial adviser, sometimes appointed by the employer. Such advice usually leads people to "balanced", "managed" or even "tracker" funds. If a "balanced" or "managed" fund gets markets wrong, the worker loses value from her or his pension. "Tracker" funds attempt to follow the market average, which is simple and cheap in rising markets but dangerous in falling markets. In the unstable market environment now prevailing, many defined contribution pensions risk direct losses.

The combination of a deep recession, trade wars, the interest cost of debt and the barrier beyond which debt cannot be repaid, all threaten conventional investment assumptions:

- For defined benefit schemes, pension deficits rise when investment values and long-term interest rates fall together, in which case severe pressure is unavoidable. This will result in lower pensions for future retirees. However, pension funds that are solvent and matching liabilities, will be unaffected.

- For defined contribution schemes, falls in values before retirement translate directly to lower pensions. After retirement, taking a pension from the fund brings continued market risk. However, taking an annuity will then bring the pension being paid within the scope of any insurance company protection.

Lower pensions lie ahead, no matter what guarantees have been given or rights accrued.

DEFINED BENEFIT PENSION PROTECTION

In the United Kingdom, there is a system for protecting these pensions when companies fail. Essentially it consists of levying other schemes, through the intermediation of the Pension Protection Fund. Pensioners of failed businesses who have already retired continue to receive their pensions but may not receive any increases. Those who worked for the failed business and have not yet retired when the company failed will receive reduced pensions, only 90% of their promised pension at retirement age, provided their pension entitlement was no more than £41,461 per annum. If they were entitled to a higher pension, their pension is capped at £37,315 (i.e. 90% of the limit of £41,461). The cap level is adjusted annually and these figures are for those retiring at age 65 in 2020. What matters to employees is the cap at the date of company failure: the cap for Carillion pensioners (Chapter 5) is lower than the current one.

Although pensions in payment are transferred to the Pension Protection Fund, those not yet in payment remain the responsibility of a company that no longer exists. Two different situations arise, according to whether there are sufficient funds to buy annuities at the reduced level (90% of promised pension up to the capped limit):

- Annuities are purchased if there are sufficient funds to do so.
- Otherwise, pension liabilities and investments are transferred to consolidators, that is to managers who specialise in handling failed schemes, acting on behalf of the Pension Protection Fund. These consolidators have their shortfalls met by the levy mechanism.

The levy mechanism charges all defined benefit schemes, whether in surplus or deficit. Those in deficit pay a higher levy to recognise their higher risk. All levies cause overhead costs to rise. The amount of investment income spent by schemes on paying their own pensions will fall, and therefore the cost of pension deficits in failed companies such as Carillion (Chapter 5) will be partly met by future pensioners of other businesses. The levy system pushes underfunded schemes further into deficit.

Defined benefit schemes generally are in deficit. According to *The Guardian* in 2017,[30] UK companies had pension deficits of £62 billion, which was about 70% of the net profits of those companies. Many of these United Kingdom schemes have been closed to new employees. In recent years, pension deficits have risen further and in 2020 were estimated at £176.3 billion net of surpluses.[31] About two-thirds of schemes are in deficit and about four-fifths are closed to new members.

PENSION INVESTMENT

Liability discounting is a technical matter for defined benefit pension schemes but valuation risk affects both types of pension and is of interest to all investors. Pension investment is a mirror of everybody's savings everywhere – excepting, perhaps, bank deposits.

The fundamental financial assets are shares, fixed interest and property. Stock (share) markets have been extraordinarily high for decades, buoyed by the flow of easy credit that has characterised the neo-liberal years. What is the future for share prices as the financial system limit bites more deeply? A prolonged 'bear' market (one in which the overall trend of prices is down) would affect every investor.

Government bonds now yield little; in many major economies, their yields are negative. Fixed interest government bonds form a capital preservation strategy but earn nothing towards paying pensions. Other types of fixed interest bring new risks:

- When a company or unsound government defaults on its bonds, there is no further income and capital is lost or reduced.
- Some index-linked bonds, such as UK indexed Gilts, index downwards as well as upwards with no minimum guarantee, so deflation can reduce both capital and income. Other index-linked securities such as US TIPS contain minimum capital guarantees.

Property prices have been driven up for years by the ready availability of credit. When economies turn down, credit becomes scarce. Commercial property of all types – shops, offices, warehouses, factories, buy-to-let houses and flats – eventually has to respond to an economic downturn. One way or another, capital values and future income streams from property will decline.

One of the characteristics of the neo-liberal decades has been the appearance of other asset types as investments: commodities, precious metals, art works, currencies. These were followed by the rise of hedge funds using derivatives to exploit the credit boom, then by private equity which took advantage of readily-available credit to acquire businesses and make them "tax efficient" by increasing debt in their capital structure. Then came the explosive growth of 'alternative investments,' including funds that enable any investor to exploit gearing (leverage) in order to turn a small rise in value into a larger rise. Debt in capital structures and debt used to attempt to achieve enhanced returns, are symptomatic of the debt-saturated nature of economies. Of course, when the underlying asset for a geared investment falls in price, gearing works in reverse by turning a small loss into a larger one. Markets have only given generous rewards for as long as central banks have successfully expanded the supply of credit.

PART THREE

HOW CAN THE WORLD ESCAPE ITS DEBT PROBLEM?

7 EXISTING IDEAS

Various ideas have circulated for how to escape the debt trap.

1. **Fiscal policy** is now being widely offered as a solution, since it is recognised that monetary policy can achieve little more. This involves deliberately increased government spending, sometimes combined with tax reductions. Governments that raise less in taxes and/or spend more, must borrow more. What is the downside?

   - Fiscal stimulus continues to increase debt, money spent on interest rises and the process adds to the amount of economic output spent on repayment. When fiscal stimulus results in additional bank lending, households and businesses borrow and the rise in spending on interest will be greater than for government's own use of the stimulus. The result is the same as if central banks directly stimulated with quantitative easing.

- It is argued that governments should borrow cheaply while interest rates are low. Government spending can be broadly classified as either on infrastructure, on public services or as transfer payments within society (pensions and benefits). Public services and transfer payments operate on a "cash in, cash out now" basis. Infrastructure spending is genuine long-term investment. When deflation occurs, today's cheap borrowing to fund infrastructure will turn out expensive in the future, because real interest rates rise as inflation turns negative.

2. **Prevent banks creating credit**: the privilege of creating private debt should be handed to governments. They would have a monopoly on credit creation just as they have a monopoly on printing banknotes.[32]

    This proposal would continue creating debt and amplifying interest. It will not work because:

- It is total debt that matters – neither the particular kind of debt nor who supplies it is important.
- Redistributing debt does not reduce its cost: compliance costs and loan losses, described in Chapter 2,

will be unaffected, unless governments impose simpler laws on themselves.

3. **Helicopter money** is another fashionable idea. As originally envisaged, it was intended to be a random distribution of cash to some of the population, financed by governments printing banknotes.

- This money ought to cause inflation. However, when there is too much debt to service, positive real interest rates cause the debt overhang to act as a *brake*.
- Why should some people be favoured with a random cash distribution and not others? This would reward some borrowers but equally would reward those with assets but no borrowing. Imagine the outcry from those borrowers who have not been so favoured.
- There is also an inherent technical problem. Handing out cash to the public only stimulates the economy if the public spend that cash, thereby creating extra demand. More likely, some of those with assets would add to their savings and many of those with debts will use their windfall either in lieu of further borrowing, or to pay down debt. Such behaviours shrink the economy instead of boosting it.

4. **Cancelling both debt and an equal amount of credit** happens on a small scale when banks write off bad debts; the cancelled credits reduce the banks' own capital. Can this be expanded?

- There is exactly the same objection as with helicopter money, substituting arbitrary selection for randomness. How will the candidates for debt cancellation be chosen and who will decide the extent of relief to be provided?

- Again, there is a technical problem. The financial structure of any bank consists of its assets, namely cash provided by owners' equity together with loans made by the bank, offset by liabilities to pay depositors and shareholders. Equity is usually 8-12% of the bank's total assets. If the bank writes off (cancels) loans it has made that, in aggregate, exceed its equity, then the bank must go bust. This is known as a solvency failure, to distinguish it from a liquidity failure (run on the bank) when a large proportion of depositors demand their money back but the bank cannot recall outstanding loans fast enough.

- To avoid destroying banks, debts would need to be reduced by directly cancelling an equal value of deposits. But which businesses or households would volunteer to have their capital or savings reduced by debt cancellation? None.

5. **Paying off world debts by liquidating assets.** We saw in Chapter 2 that world assets are $317 trillion and world debts $244 trillion. It ought to be possible, therefore, to liquidate $244 trillion of financial assets to pay off all those debts, leaving the world with assets worth only $73 trillion. This reduced capital base would incur no debt interest. However:

- Governments would have to agree between them how to allocate forced sales and repayments, to allow for disparities in the ratio of assets to debt in each country. Those whose countries have insufficient assets to pay down all their own debts would need to be subsidised by others.
- Every government in the world would then have to decide how to reduce assets fairly, so that all their country's debt could be paid off. Investors, businesses, and savers would be left with severely reduced capital and savings.

6. **Taxing wealth to pay down debt** has limited benefit, as shown in Chapter 4. Piketty's proposal was restricted to paying down government debt, not total debt.

7. **Debt to equity conversion** would make Islamic banking the mainstream model, replacing debt-based lending by equity risk-sharing. There are some positive aspects: business creation and expansion would no longer bring interest costs. Houses could be financed by shared equity, with the owners gradually buying out other investors over the years, if they wished. Financial leverage would disappear, ending some financial engineering tricks that transfer wealth rather than create it.

Nothing is simple in economics and there are also downsides to converting debt to equity:

- Retired people relying on deposit interest to pay for their cost of living would have their bank interest replaced by uncertain dividends – sometimes leading to no income at all.
- Banks would become giant investment funds and therefore risk-averse savers would lose pound for pound, dollar for dollar, repayment of their capital as deposits are converted into equity stakes.
- The effect would be to raise howls of protest that people's savings were being confiscated in order to release existing borrowers from their responsibilities.
- Capital is global and therefore all nations would have to agree to make the identical change at the same time.

8. Government debt should only be repaid slowly, if at all. The United Kingdom has given the world a lesson in the social disruption caused by austerity. The original plan was a five-year target for reduced public debt, since elongated to nine years. Even so, the plan did not stop the rise in total debt, of which government debt forms only part. Cutting too quickly took spending power out of the British economy. Avoiding tax rises left those dependent on public services and welfare support – the poorest – struggling most as social services and welfare support were cut back.

Suppose a country decided to repay all its debt very slowly instead of rapidly, with repayments only occurring in growth years and at a barely-noticeable rate:

- It would take decades. Consequences would include shrinking corporate activity and reduced consumer spending as less credit is acquired, or even some debt is repaid. Living standards would suffer.
- Since debt is a global problem, would other countries join in? Any country trying to repay debt by shrinking its economy would also reduce its trade. Countries that chose not to participate would still find their economies and trade contracting, but less than the contraction in the austere country. Whether austerity is pursued slowly or quickly is therefore

irrelevant: the policy automatically causes *relative* decline.

- Voters will not countenance near-permanent austerity and a change of governing party would probably lead to immediate abandonment of such a policy.

9. **Expanding Special Drawing Rights** at the International Monetary Fund (IMF) is also suggested as a possible solution. Special Drawing Rights (SDR) are an artificial creation. They are a partial successor to the 'Bancor' designed by Keynes but never implemented.[33] The IMF periodically adjusts its members' contributions (also called quotas) to reflect their relative size. Although the IMF does support countries having balance of payments difficulties, it is primarily focused on donor needs by size.

- SDRs increased following the credit crunch from about 21.4 billion to 204 billion (SDR 204 billion is equivalent to US$ 281 billion), so they are already part of the problem. Issued in proportion to IMF contributions, they mainly benefit developed countries.[34]

- Expanding Special Drawing Rights merely pushes the credit creation problem deeper into the financial system. Resulting loans add to the debt burden on recipient countries and are therefore deflationary.

10. Abandoning economic stimulus completely is another theoretical solution. It would take the world back to pre-Keynesian economics:

- Recessions would purge economies and therefore more businesses would fail.
- Neither governments nor central banks would be able to expand the money supply. Credit would become a finite resource.
- The existing cost of interest would be little changed. Nothing would be achieved towards reducing the proportion of economic output spent on interest, although growth in the cost of interest may be ameliorated.

NONE OF THE 'IDEAS' CAN WORK

The above proposals appear occasionally in the media, offered as a "solution" to economic stagnation. As the summary table (Table 6) shows, they either make the problem worse, have inherent faults or create conflict between those with assets and those who have only debt. The common-sense view, that a debt problem cannot be solved by creating more, remains unchallengeable. The uncomfortable truth is that credit can easily be created, thereby creating artificial wealth, but it is difficult to reverse the process:

Table 6 Debt reduction solutions that do not work

Proposed 'solution'	Increase cost of interest?	Create conflict?	Inherent problem(s)?
Modern Monetary Theory (Chapter 4)	Yes		
Fiscal policy	Yes		
Governments create debt	Yes		
Helicopter money		Yes	Yes
Debt cancellation		Yes	Yes
Sell assets		Yes	Yes
Taxing wealth		Yes	Yes
Debt to equity conversion		Yes	Yes
Slow debt repayment		Yes	Yes
Expand SDRs			Yes
Pre-Keynesian economics			Yes

8 TACKLING THE COST OF INTEREST TO SOCIETY

Administered interest rates set by Western central banks are at an extremely low level. The 'spread' between the retail cost of credit and these rates is wide, as shown by Figure 1 (Chapter 1).

The long fall in interest paid to depositors started around 1982. As central bank borrowing rates and government bond yields have declined towards zero, those charged by banks to borrowers (businesses and households) have stayed at high levels. Although there are variations between countries and also in the mix of debt types when one country is compared to another, the decline in actual rates paid has been slow to non-existent nearly everywhere. Except for governments, borrowing money is expensive.

However, this is *not* a story about greedy bankers. Rather, it is the tale of governments imposing ever-increasing overheads on the banking system. This started with extra regulation in the 1980s and has increased steadily ever since. The order in which regulations appeared was:

- Basel Committee Capital Standards (1988, revised 2004, 2011, 2017);
- Financial Action Task Force (Proceeds of Crime, 1989); then
- FATCA (United States Foreign Account Tax Compliance Act, 2013); and finally
- the Common Reporting Standard (CRS, 2014) developed by the OECD (Organisation for Economic Cooperation and Development).

The Basel Committee sets standards for bank capital, allowing for the different types of business conducted by banks and their individual risk profiles. Capital should be sufficient for the bank to stay in business even when high levels of loan losses occur.

Internationally, the Financial Action Task Force (FATF) has made escalating and expensive demands for banks to hunt for criminal proceeds, money used for terrorist financing and money not properly taxed.

FATCA is American legislation that restricts banks wishing to settle in US dollars to only having trading relationships with other FATCA-compliant banks. Since all US dollar transactions are ultimately settled in New York and the US dollar is the pre-eminent trading currency, FATCA has effectively imposed some American banking and taxation regulation on the world.

CRS now enables over 100 jurisdictions to exchange tax information automatically, thereby allowing participating governments to tax everything they wish. The United States remains outside CRS because FATCA allows the USA to demand information from other countries, although the USA does not reciprocate.

Countries also impose licensing requirements on all banks operating within their jurisdiction. The objectives are to balance economic activity with consumer and business protection. The rules relate to capital requirements, conduct of business and depositor protection. Licensing requirements are themselves complex, although they are largely standardised across the European Union and three European Economic Area countries. The United Kingdom also requires major banks to ring-fence their retail activities from other banking business; there are political demands in the USA to reimpose separation of wholesale and retail banking activities, which was the case from 1933-99 when the Glass-Steagall Act was in force.

Regulators and tax authorities have imposed large fines often enough to scare banks into overkill compliance, which may be unproductive. Are so many individual regulatory bodies required? Surely this creates more cost for the world to spend on its banking system.

Here is a simple example of how change could be tackled. Every person conducting financial transactions meets frequent demands for identity evidence. Large banks already have access to international identity databases. Why not allow all financial institutions to use these, require the database proprietors to record all checks electronically and provide them to enforcement agencies possessing a warrant? A simple computer record could then replace endless certifying and filing copies of passports and identity cards. However, does society want the loss of privacy and security risk that such a centralised system introduces, or would we rather pay more for banking services?

If these aspects can be confronted and banking costs reduced, it would hopefully allow banks to reduce overheads and pass savings on to the end consumer.

PART FOUR

THE PANDEMIC AND THE FINANCIAL SYSTEM LIMIT

9 IMPACT OF THE PANDEMIC

ECONOMIES AND BORROWING

The economic effect of the pandemic varies with the resilience of individual nations. Those that had inadequate preparations, were slow going into lockdown and also slow vaccinating, now have to face hesitant recoveries. These countries may record increases in debt arising from economic support to their people.

Although government debt is seen as cheap, countries that have encouraged banks to support their economies, and countries where businesses and households have borrowed more, will have added to the cost of economic output spent on interest. The combination of a higher numerator (interest expense) and smaller denominator (economic output) will cause the wasted output to rise above one-fifth. Paying more interest on reduced economic output points towards global inability to afford debt on a Puerto Rican scale.

As for Britain, before the 2016 EU referendum I made a private forecast that, if the country voted Leave, the United Kingdom would eventually suffer a bigger decline in output than other European nations when the next recession arrived. Leaving the European single market will now lead Britain to a slower, less effective recovery from the pandemic than the rest of Europe.

ONGOING EFFECT OF THE VIRUS

Nobody knows how long the infection will continue, nor whether there will be further economic disruption. This raises various questions. First, can coronavirus be eradicated by lockdowns or by 'test, trace and isolate'? Unfortunately, not all countries will apply as stringent restrictions to their people as the Chinese authorities did in Wuhan. Eradication by isolation is unlikely.

Second, if not eradicated, can the virus be reduced to a very low level and kept at a low level? Again, unlikely, as different countries have conflicting priorities. Some refuse all measures, others are selective in their chosen policies and implementation.

Third, can a vaccine or combination of vaccines succeed in preventing infection? Probably, but not necessarily. As with influenza, the virus may mutate constantly and remain with us.

And fourth, how long will it take to produce and distribute enough to vaccinate the majority of world population? 2022 seems a realistic target.

Recovery will also be affected by the state of health care. Several African, Asian and Latin American countries are short of doctors. The USA, almost alone among developed nations, lacks universal provision. Many governments will now face demands for improved health care provision.

Poor parts of the world will face the prospect of famine because farmers infected by the virus were unable to plant crops, but even wealthy countries may develop a hunger problem: in Britain, use of food charities is rising steeply. Africa has to contend with locust swarms. There may be more deaths arising from delays in existing vaccination programmes than were averted by the lockdown.

Business as usual?

Forecasts of economic loss need to consider increased interest costs. Some forecasts assume a return to 'business as usual'. Even if this were possible, 'usual' would not be achieved until 2022 at the earliest. At least three years (2020, 2021 and 2022) would be affected by severe economic damage. More likely, 'business as we knew it' will never return, because people's behaviour will change. Under financial pressure to sustain home and family, old norms of economic behaviour will be swept away. War, revolution, economic collapse and plague have always been closely linked and history shows that they do change behaviour.[35] If the virus mutates faster than vaccines can be found, there will be a constant drain on global finance.

One economic forecast can reliably be identified now. The pandemic will be deflationary. Isolated examples of price rises will occur transiently, notably in the food chain and transport, but overall the loss of economic output combined with loss of financial resources in capital markets (including reduced future pensions, Chapter 6) will see price levels fall, although in ways impossible to predict with certainty. Deflation in the 1930s followed a collapse in confidence after the 1929 crash.

RESILIENCE

During the neo-liberal years, price competition was severe and businesses chose the cheapest source of goods. This fuelled the rapid growth of manufacturing in many Asian countries, which collectively became the world's workshop. Now that long supply chains and single-sources of key components appear riskier, a more varied manufacturing supply chain will emerge. The Indian government is planning to exploit this opportunity with more infrastructure investment to attract Western manufacturers. Turkey has similar ambitions.

The digital world needs reliable safe infrastructure. The internet has coped well with data transfer demand but criminals have found more opportunities. There are perennial concerns about system complexity, driven by failures such as credit card authorisation and disrupted transfers between bank accounts. Software and hardware have acquired layers of additional complexity.

Whereas manufacturing industries are now attempting to spread risk, complex digital infrastructure *concentrates* risk.

PEOPLE AND WORK

Destitution is spreading. Families who have lost their breadwinners to coronavirus are hit hardest. Hunger may be avoided only in advanced countries having either generous welfare benefits for all residents, or a strong charitable tradition.

Poorer countries in the world often have only two main sources of foreign income. One is cheap labour and this will be damaged by lower levels of consumer spending in western countries plus businesses manufacturing closer to home. Their second source of income is money sent home by citizens who have moved to wealthier countries to take unwanted jobs. The value of such remittances has dropped as the pandemic spread.

There will be more unemployment everywhere. Business collapses caused by the pandemic are still at an early stage. Some businesses will survive by shrinking their activities and laying off employees. In April 2020, the International Labour Organisation reported that 1.6 billion people could already be unemployed, but every such forecast is liable to be out of date in weeks.

Some of those thrown out of work will increase their debt. Short-term interest and repayment waivers will come to an end. House prices will fall as families try to escape debt by scaling down or selling to rent. Banks may become reluctant landlords.

Changing values

Before the pandemic, the world was on a debt treadmill, bringing high stress levels to those in work and those without work. Do we really value such lifestyles? Surveys showed that a significant number were dissatisfied with their jobs. Changing lifestyles will be part of the coming behavioural change. In developed societies, people will probably value community more and consumerism less. In *The Greatest Crash* I discussed the possibility of communism and Islam merging as Commumislam.

Young people are worst affected by the employment threat. Britain is an outlier because its young have lost their right to work in 31 other European countries. After the financial crisis of 2008/9 and the health crisis of 2020, the young are even more likely to demand serious action on climate change. Governments need to tread carefully, look after the young, and even consider if public priorities and governance structures are appropriate.

"WHATEVER IT TAKES"

This is a dangerous political mantra. Extensive borrowing and depressed economic activity have brought the world closer to the financial system limit. How much more total debt can societies absorb? *Before* the pandemic, the world as a whole was just over half-way to achieving Puerto Rican default conditions.

Tax rises are inevitable, but they also impact on economic activity. Taking more in income or expenditure taxes from the middle classes when the economic background is deflationary will cause households and businesses to reduce their discretionary spending. Consumption will then decline, leading to reduced business activity. Chapters 4 and 7 discussed the problem of taxing capital. Wealth taxes can help a little, particularly if they redistribute purchasing power rather than take purchasing power out of the economy, but they are not a magical solution. Lower-tax societies may adopt higher taxes to transfer resources from the affluent to those whose skills are critical to a functioning society but hitherto have been undervalued. However, tax rises to fund governments may do little more than replace revenues lost as a result of reduced economic activity.

Past tax rises have sometimes been counterproductive, as were the Lawson and Brown raids on pension funds that started UK defined benefit pensions on the road to underfunding.[36]

United Kingdom pundits argue that government borrowing was 250% of GDP in 1945 and therefore pandemic borrowing of around 100% of GDP is nothing unusual. This ignores the vast growth in household and business credit in post-war years. Many households and businesses are constrained by their present debt-service costs. Such costs did not exist in 1945.

Those with reasonably secure incomes will spend less and save more. Others with debts will spend less to repay some debt. This leads to a paradox, because economic statistics treat debt repayment as saving. Demand for credit will decline, just as banks become even more selective about who they lend money to. People will be less willing to take on debt and keener to pay it down. No amount of Keynesian stimulus can force credit on reluctant households and businesses when they turn averse to borrowing. Nor can banks be forced to lend to debt-saturated consumers and businesses, even with government guarantees against default. Borrowing to invest, for example in property, will go out of fashion.

These factors will exacerbate and prolong the economic decline, since less debt means less money in circulation. They also act as a brake on official attempts to promote renewed growth. Less money in circulation combined with paying down debt, rather than accumulating more, will prolong the recession.

The mantra "whatever it takes" has been used to justify a rapid increase in global debt to fight every economic downturn. Quantitative easing (monetising debt), fiscal policy and all the other tricks that amount to borrowing more from the future, will not work. Austerity has also failed.

Facing a serious deflation, the world is in a debt trap resulting from decades of credit expansion, now deepened by the pandemic.

THE KEYNESIAN FAILURE

This takes us to the central failure of Keynesian stimulus: slow accretion of debt gradually thwarts any benefit from stimulus.

Private comments made by Keynesian economists in response to the first edition of this book revealed how deep the assumption "all stimulus is good" runs in our society. I was presented with four main arguments:

1. If people cannot afford their debts they should go bust.

2. Interest rates are so low that debt service costs do not matter.

3. Debt is balanced by equal credits, so net debt is zero.

4. Interest is just a transfer from one group of people to another group.

The first three arguments completely miss the point. Did Keynes intend that vast numbers of the population should go bankrupt as a result of his policies? Of course not. The side-effect of cumulative interest costs simply never arose, because debt levels were so low in the 1930s. Neither Keynes nor his disciples foresaw the eventual creation of unaffordable debt nearly a century later. This cannot be dismissed by arguing that debits and credits balance out or that interest is just a transfer payment.

My interest rate calculations in Chapter 2 were estimates based on 2018 data. There is an urgent need for more understanding of the effect of the cost of total interest on our society. As footnote 9 to Chapter 2 shows,[9] statistics about interest costs show some inconsistency and, in the United

Kingdom, are collected for a different purpose than burden calculation.

Continuing with economic stimulus policies will gradually cause more economic output to be spent on interest: more money wasted to keep the edifice of credit afloat.

10 DEFLATION

Deflation happens when demand collapses and therefore prices fall. The deflation that, in my view, is now inevitable will be caused by excess debt resulting from prolonged financial stimulus. This is a greater challenge than financing the economic stimulus used to keep economies alive during the pandemic.

Governments have slowly built a debt trap for the world. Central banks have done their handiwork, but in a system designed by politicians. No one living individual can be blamed for this group think.

The real burden of debt will be borne by businesses and families. Actions of governments and their agencies to increase the supply of credit are slowly worsening the economic environment. Prior to the pandemic, the extra credit flowed into stock market bubbles, national bankruptcies such as

Puerto Rico, corporate bankruptcies such as Carillion and social bankruptcy through rising inequality.

THE CONTRAST BETWEEN INFLATION AND DEFLATION

Until inflation appeared in the 1960s, a fixed income such as a pension was desirable. Two decades of inflation then destroyed the value of fixed incomes. People learned from experience that fixed incomes were to be avoided. Governments learned the contrasting lesson, that inflation eroded the true cost of their debt.

Deflation has the opposite effect to inflation. Having a fixed income is brilliant, but deflation piles hidden costs onto borrowing. People now have to learn (or, perhaps, be taught) that borrowing becomes more expensive over time even when it appears to be cheap initially.

On 4th June 2020 I watched a television report of the economic effect of the pandemic. It stated that the British government could borrow for ten years at 0.2%, implying that the deficit caused by the pandemic would not matter.

This report did not consider the inability of people to service extensive debts, particularly at the consumer costs noted in Chapters 1 and 2. Even if the deflation rate is as little as 1% a year for five years and then somehow deflation ceases at that lower price level with stable prices returning, for the second half of the ten year term the British government would have a real cost of 5.2% annually on such borrowing. This is the result of positive real interest rates for borrowers.

The news programme continued with an interview featuring two economists. One subscribed to Modern Monetary Theory, which this book examined in Chapter 4. She said the Federal Reserve could create as much money as the US government needed. The other interviewee was an economic historian who took a broader perspective about debt.

This news report demonstrated how people need to grasp the concept of the financial system limit. It showed that academia needs to think broadly about the concepts described in this book. Even informed professionals do not understand the debt trap that the world is in.

There is a technical measure of the British recession ahead. Under inflationary conditions, the yield on offer in the government bond market rises with longer maturities. Insurance companies and pension funds have very long timescales and dominate purchases of these longer maturities. It is possible to get a feel for the position now by considering an identical coupon (the rate of interest per £100 nominal) at different maturities. In the UK Gilt market, the 4.25% coupon serves this function. At 29th May 2020 the seven year 4.25% coupon could be bought for an income yield of 3.23% and a loss if held to maturity of 24.0%. At the other extreme, the Gilt with the same coupon of 4.25% maturing nineteen years later offered an income yield of only 2.24% and a loss to maturity of 47.27%. Investors are prepared to pay much more for what appears at first sight to be worse value. This is the market's way of anticipating a serious recession and even lower real interest rates.

News programmes report events. Redundancies so far form the first wave. As with the pandemic, a second wave of business closures can be expected. Take, for example, the theoretical model of a property developer with significant bank borrowings, facing withheld rents and vacant offices or shops that cannot be easily let to new tenants. Bank borrowings were a classic way for property developers to increase the capital value of their businesses. A small amount of the developer's own capital could fund a much bigger development when enlarged with bank borrowing. The second wave will include a repeat of the 1975 experience, when both property companies and obscure financiers collapsed. Rents will fall, banks take losses, and credit shrink further. This is how deflation can progress. It's dangerous, because debt costs drive living standards down, increasing poverty. If a spiral of decline develops, then defaults will rise, threatening the financial system as we know it.

Consumer spending is likely to settle at lower levels as people choose not to add to debt, or even to pay it down. Businesses face higher costs to build resilience into supply chains and to handle climate change. The combination will result in fewer goods and services bought by households. Volume shrinkage at higher prices may be a feature of the coming deflation. For example, there will probably be fewer flights at higher prices.

CONTRADICTIONS

There are difficult contradictions in the present economic and political situations that need to be better understood:

1. Refusing to stimulate our way out of recession is seen as foolish. Yet adding to the money already wasted on interest is equally so. The choice seems to be: foolishness now versus deferred foolishness when the interest cost has mounted further.

2. Existing policies no longer work. Instead of debating stimulus versus austerity or lower interest rates versus fighting inflation, economists and politicians need to think about how to get private sector debt levels and their associated interest costs down.

3. Public services, taxation, public borrowing and regulation are in a four-way contradiction: it is impossible to meet the requirements of all four. Taxation incurs deadweight costs of administration, while public expenditure

encourages marginal use of scarce resources. Politicians like to boast about public services but realise that rising taxes and increased regulation are unpopular.

This political statement appeared in *The Observer*:[37]

"There is now real concern about the long-term impact of quantitative easing which, coupled with austerity, has led to rocketing asset prices, falling wages and rising inequality. Those with access to central bank largesse have been enriched as the prices of assets have risen; while those without assets and dependent on earnings have suffered as incomes have fallen in real terms."

The essence of this quotation is that neo-liberalism has failed. In my view, neo-liberalism is just the political gloss to hide the ongoing failure of economic policy. In order to recognise the need for new thinking, policy-makers must accept the concepts set out in the first three chapters and how these three factors are linked by positive real interest rates. Only then can a serious evaluation of effective future courses of action be considered.

The cost of servicing existing debt prevents expansionary monetary policy from having any lasting beneficial effect. There is a short-term benefit from escaping the latest crisis, which is nullified by the long-term real cost of additional ongoing debt interest payments. The central banking cycle exacerbates the existing failure, but does so with a delay of perhaps a decade. Politicians with typically four to six year terms of office are therefore tempted to fix the immediate problem caused by each downturn, while damning the future. Overall, the central banking cycle postpones hitting the debt ceiling but makes the limit bite more severely when recession next comes round. Debts created to fight the economic shock of the pandemic will enhance the *next* recession. The weight of private sector debt paying higher interest rates accentuates these barriers to growth.

Economics does not currently appear to recognise these issues, although some economists, as in the example quoted above, do see that conventional wisdom has failed. Political wisdom is in an even worse condition. The old left-right divide sets public services against private exploitation, state provision versus privatisation. There are two new divides. One sets those with an instinct towards alliances and communal solutions against the doctrine of the individual and the allure of free markets. The second sets those with assets and income against those saddled with debt: students, homeowners, even businesses owned by some private equity financiers.

Traditional solutions no longer work; the trickle-down theory and market obsession of neo-liberalism have achieved little. These schools of thought are now irrelevant to the world's financial problems.

FAILING POLICIES

The authorities are fighting the depression caused by the pandemic with the failed formula of the past forty years.

No doubt conventional policy-makers will dream up further successors to quantitative easing (QE). This policy was adopted when simple expansion of bank lending no longer delivered rapid results for political gain. QE has contributed to the severe social problems the world now faces. Even government borrowing at low rates adds to the debt burden and cost of interest, either by creating more private debt, or by pushing inflation down further thereby adding to the real cost of money.

Governments applied Keynesian economics steadily after the end of World War II. As a result, recessions were mild and economic growth almost continuous. This lasted until the cumulative cost of paying interest on borrowed money overwhelmed the benefits of adding to the money supply, which was a gradual change from the 1980s onward. People look back fondly to the days when expansionary credit policies brought economic growth and wish such times would return. Few understand how unaffordable debt, caused by past monetary expansion, now curtails any benefit from further stimulus.

The internet has enabled the sharing economy, making services such as car sharing and short-term home rental technically feasible. But the economic rationale for the sharing economy partly depends on incomes being under pressure. The sharing economy tells us how pressured the economic background is. Resources are shared to get costs down. People have to take low-paid jobs in the gig economy to survive.

In future years, more economies will struggle. Think of Japan, where for the last thirty years the cycle of monetary expansion, fiscal expansion and political reform has delivered a series of policies that have been unable to get Japan booming. Politicians will prove powerless, debt problems and destitution will be more common, incomes will be under pressure, asset prices will fall more than they rise. Pricing power – the ability of businesses to set price levels of their own choosing – has now disappeared and this loss affects most industries. Price competition leads consumers to demand the cheapest then complain, often on the internet, if the quality or service is less than perfect.

Few businesses can nowadays escape the effects of regulation, stricter liability and costly legal requirements. Overheads have risen as a result of control by government or its agencies, excessive record keeping requirements and hidden banking costs. Has anybody measured them?

THE POLITICAL SYSTEM LIMIT

The financial system limit brings with it a political system limit. With the failure of monetary policy and impending failure of fiscal policy, there will no longer be any easy tools available to politicians to produce quick fixes before facing electorates. Managing the electoral cycle using economic tools no longer delivers results: the policy lever marked 'expansion' no longer works.

The United Kingdom made a signal error in blaming Europe for its troubles. Sure, regulatory overhead is too high but some of this was caused by the British bureaucracy's habit of "gold-plating" everything coming out of Brussels. Some directives had been drafted by Britain in the first place. Gold plating may even have contributed to Britain's poor productivity. From Europe, Britain was once seen as having a Rolls-Royce administration, or put more realistically, as being willing to pour resources into administration. The habit of writing excessive rules is more British than European and this trend will doubtless mushroom with the United Kingdom outside the European Union.

Developed nations are afflicted by the cult of uniformity and loss of knowledge. Take the diesel motor car as a recent example. Politicians and bureaucrats promoted its supposed fuel efficiency, encouraging it through regulation and taxation. Modern diesel engines have much lower Carbon

Dioxide (CO_2) emissions than comparable petrol engines. But now we know that particulates and Nitrogen Dioxide (NO_2), both of which arise from diesel motors, are injurious to health; the environment operates in a complex stasis in which solving one problem can make another worse. There is another lesson to be learned here too: that centralised decision-making is vulnerable to elementary mistakes.

The loss of knowledge stems from promoting the opinions of those who lack understanding. We live in a media dominated world. Some media confuse lack of bias with equal treatment of different points of view, thereby giving undue weight to emotions, mistaken arguments and sheer distortions of facts promoted by minorities or by scheming politicians. Few people recognise truly original thought any more, preferring to follow their own predispositions and prejudices. Society lives for the moment, with little strategic vision.

Since every decision involves making difficult choices, the public should be included in the political process, not dictated to by remote authority. Britain's highly centralised bureaucracy is institutionally unsuited to this approach. HM Treasury's reluctance to link particular taxes to corresponding expenditures is inappropriate for a deflationary world. Rather, people should vote on whether they want to pay taxes for specific purposes. The public must face up to the real issues and make their voices heard; Whitehall, Brussels and the Beltway do not have all the answers.

Politicians need to understand that there are no magic answers, no policy levers that can solve the dilemma of 'stimulate and add to stagnation in a decade, versus do not stimulate and risk immediate stagnation.'

What led politicians to make our debt problems worse? Economics originated as a social and political science but has somehow lost its way buried in the detail of micro-economics. The old formula of 'stimulate your way out of recession' worked when debt levels were much lower, nowhere near the feasible limits, and therefore credit could expand without anyone considering the consequences. As noted, for a period that ended nearly forty years ago, that expansion caused negative real interest rates. Now, after seventy-five years of the post-war consensus, in which every recession has been neutered by economic stimulus, the economic cycle driven by central banks keeps bumping up against the financial system limit.

A MODEST ALTERNATIVE TO DEBT

State ownership of industry has acquired an unfortunate reputation. From the Labour government of 1945 until Thatcher came to power in 1979, Britain pursued a "mixed economy" in which the State owned significant industries. In true British fashion, these were run as a series of centralised "command and control" bureaucracies that satisfied few.

One immediate way to reduce the dependence on debt would be to allow governments to raise new money neither by taxation, nor by borrowing, but instead by selling shares in new ventures to the public. This is not the same as the United Kingdom's public dividend capital, by which the centralised state holds equity in state businesses. Nor is it privatisation of existing state services by selling shares to the public or creating new state-funded contracts. Rather, new businesses would be founded to direct people's savings to good causes, professionally managed. The role of government would be as an enabler, to sponsor creation of suitable companies. Voters would have management influence in how such finance should be used through annual general meetings. This would move the emphasis from money creation to productive use of existing savings. But it would still be a drop in the ocean of world debt. It would be the antithesis of debt-obsessed private equity.

There is an urgent need to support economies devastated by coronavirus. Here are two examples. Both would allow some replacement of debt finance and therefore contribute, albeit minutely, to holding off the financial system limit:

1. Why not raise some development aid to less developed countries as equity by public subscription? The aid business can operate at arms length to government in

competition with the private aid foundations, answerable directly to its shareholders.

2. In Europe, people could support the particularly badly damaged economies with equity development funding instead of loans. There should be a general improvement condition, for example to rise two or three places in the World Bank's "Ease of doing business" study within a set period of time. Such an arrangement would have three benefits:

- European citizens would be directly involved in their own continent's economic recovery;
- the weaker EU member states would be encouraged to improve their efficiency; and
- objections to debt finance would be lessened. No increase in the waste of economic output on interest, no dispute between the German constitutional court and the European Central Bank.

EVOLUTIONARY CHANGE

In the days when the early Italian bankers invented debit and credit, there was no European Commission, Federal government or British regulator to lay down detailed prescriptive rules. Nowadays, politicians announce their demands, then set retinues of bureaucrats to implement their grandiose projects. The bureaucrats write detailed proposals, 'consult' on how the detail will work to ensure a degree of practicality, then write legislation to implement their design.

The entire structure of standards, rules, regulations and delegated bodies making rules, acts to prevent evolution and reinforce conformity. As bureaucratic institutions have grown in importance, so conformity has entrenched group think. This is the nature of our society. All the gears follow their cogs but the assembled whole can be a complete nonsense. Only through diversity can there be any hope of adapting to change but diversity is unwanted. Group think will flourish until the power of standards-setters and bureaucracies is curtailed. Government functions delegated to monopoly state agencies, the strength of lobby groups and vulnerability of all political systems to pressure, the sheer volume of noise in the media and on the internet, the immediacy of the demands of daily life, all combine to make our collective understanding somewhat limited and our memories short.

Society segregates policy-makers into separate silos that barely understand one another's thinking and do not communicate. Prior to the credit crunch, banks ignored prudential judgment about future bad debts because accounting standards specified detailed rules, rather than encouraging accountants to assess the dynamics and risks of the whole business. Accountants are not unique in facing such demands: other professions have also extended skill and judgment with codified requirements imposed on practitioners in the name of 'standards' or 'quality' or (in the public sector) 'targets.' Auditing accounts has become a matter of choosing which standards to apply, then checking that the standards have been followed. The standards are sacred.

The more rules that are made, the worse the problem becomes. Why? Because rules ossify the ruled and prevent evolution. According to Dr Hugo Bänziger writing in 2010,[38] the then forthcoming revised Basel rules for bank capital requirements would prompt every bank simultaneously to raise capital or reduce lending when the economic cycle next turns down.

The more governments outsource responsibility for the economic health of nations, the more delegated bodies there will be to impose their own onerous sets of rules. More banking overhead will follow but the common good will not be served by driving up total interest costs.

For alternatives to the present debt-based financial system to emerge, bureaucratic design and excessive standards must be constrained from further growth. Then some other kind of financial system might evolve, rendering the financial system limit less significant. Separation of debit and credit invented by the early Italian bankers has reached the end of its useful life. The challenge is to maintain the protections of the present system while providing an environment that encourages alternatives.

AND SO?

Authors who drive ideas forward are often expected to propose next steps, or perhaps prescribe what should be done. There are no easy answers to the problem of deflation caused by excessive levels of debt. The priority should be to stop making the situation worse. Beyond this, two points can be recognised:

1. Limited immediate relief may only be possible through redistributive taxation and simplifying compliance demands on banks.

2. Experiments should be carried out with subscription by the people, to development aid and economic support.

These points will only have a minor effect on the deflationary debt trap the world faces. The tragedy is that the authorities do not admit to the trap. The farce, that their policies worsen it.

Academics could do much more to educate about deflation, by adopting the concepts in this book. Existing theories such as the supposed tax efficiency of debt should be quietly abandoned.

While I was writing the first draft of this chapter, *The Economist* published an article[39] exploring current economic theories about debt. The theory that government debt crowds out productive debt featured in it, as did Modern Monetary Theory. But what exactly qualifies as productive debt? And why is government debt *not* productive? These are meaningless diversions. Total world debt is what matters but the aggregate cost of interest and its relation to economic output was not even mentioned. Neither was the inability to expand debt to infinity, nor existence of a central banking economic cycle.

The *Financial Times* then published an opinion article that correctly noted the ratio of total world debt to economic output but also omitted to identify the same issues. The author thought that transparency would be the key to controlling debt.[6] Instead of describing the wrong kind of debt, an approach this book rejected in Chapter 7, the article suggested that the world's debt problems arise from the wrong way of looking at debt. This book proposes that the **right** way of looking at it is to measure interest cost on total debt in relation to economic output.

The coronavirus pandemic will be seized upon by the commentariat as the 'cause' of this economic crisis and conveniently scapegoated by politicians. The truth is that a deep recession and consequential financial upset was inevitable in a world that could not resolve the conflict between stimulus and austerity, a world that remained addicted to debt, a world that refused to admit the limit to the growth of debt caused by the cost of servicing it. The central banking economic cycle is a crucial element in this depression. Every crisis – think of the dot com bust and credit crunch as well as coronavirus – results in panic measures to extend economic stimulus. These measures inevitably add to the debt burden and the deflationary forces in the global economy, thereby bringing the financial system limit closer.

The debt-based financial system as we know it has run its course. The whole world is now over half way to default. Whatever replacement to debt emerges, the world must ask: do we wish to compound economic and political upsets by continuing to expand the supply of credit? Are short-term benefits worth the longer-term cost?

I have long subscribed to the view that the policy of constantly borrowing from the future would ultimately prove unsustainable and therefore some sort of debt reckoning would lie ahead. By throwing the entire world into deep recession, the coronavirus pandemic has brought the prospect of serious deflation closer.

Much deeper issues about the sort of society we wish to be will undoubtedly come into focus in the next few years. The very existence of the financial system limit needs to be part of such thinking. Academia has apparently failed to see how serious the debt problem is, instead producing irrelevant theories that miss the severity of the debt pile. Do we have to wait for most of the world to face Puerto Rican debt conditions before anyone notices? The theories in the first three chapters now need urgent assimilation.

POSTSCRIPT: BRITAIN'S REAL DEBT PROBLEM

As countries recover from the pandemic and regain some of their lost growth, sluggish performance caused by the financial system limit will return. In addition, the United Kingdom economy will be further weakened by Brexit.

The Resolution Foundation have described this decade as challenging for the UK.[40] Their report mentions that businesses and consumers are constrained by debt, but also refers to debt as "over 100% of GDP." This repeats the common error of failing to clearly distinguish government from total debt, since private debt is about three times this.[41]

Brexit has already caused economic shrinkage.[42] Statistics are misquoted to promote spurious advantages, as these two examples show:

1. New trade agreement benefits have been publicised counting existing trade values in agreements rolled over from EU membership, making them appear far more valuable.[43]

2. UK trade with non-EU countries was growing in the last fifteen years because the EU negotiated many agreements, to the United Kingdom's benefit.

Official statistics suggest that United Kingdom GDP will shrink permanently by up to 4%. Lost fish sales are harsh for the fishing industry but trivial in relation to the whole economy. The loss of some farming may be more substantial. The loss of financial services business is significant and unrecognised. The loss of cross-border rights to practise many other services, for example entertainment, was entirely unnecessary.[44] British services sold to Europe accounted for 8% of UK GDP before the Brexit referendum. Services need to be delivered locally on local standards so much of these will be lost. All these are additional to the well-documented problems of extra trade bureaucracy and closure of smaller businesses selling goods to Europe. Therefore permanent economic contraction is likely to follow.

Over a period of twelve years, this continuing loss of 4% of GDP every year will amount to a total of half a year's economic output. Recovering from this will require a ten-year total of roughly £1,000 bn of new (not double counted) trade.

This means that Britain has to sign new trade agreements providing an aggregate gain of £100 bn per annum immediately. The prospective gains from all new agreements are liable to be a small fraction of this. The cumulative benefit is unlikely to ever make good the lost European trade. The entirely new agreement with Australia is officially estimated to be worth 0.02% of UK GDP, i.e. about £400m per annum: it is immaterial. America will extract a significant concession in terms of its agricultural produce and may be the greater beneficiary of a UK-USA agreement since the UK currently runs a surplus with America. China is out of political favour for now. Previous negotiations with India have failed twice because India insists on free movement rights. What is left? The latest (perhaps last) hope is the Comprehensive and Progressive Agreement for Trans-Pacific Partnership (CPTPP).

CPTPP members are: Australia, Brunei, Canada, Chile, Japan, Malaysia, Mexico, New Zealand, Peru, Singapore, and Vietnam, all situated around the Pacific rim. The United Kingdom already has agreements with seven of these eleven countries and is finalising agreements with Australia and New Zealand. Only Brunei and Malaysia offer completely new opportunities. Brunei's population is half-a-million, GDP about USD 12 bn. Malaysia's population is 32.7 million, GDP about USD 364 bn. How is any new trade agreement with two faraway countries having 33 million population going to replace lost trade with our 448 million European neighbours, forty times their economic size with GDP of USD 15 trn? What can be sold to them? The proposition is ridiculous.[45]

A shrinking economy makes it harder for over-borrowed consumers and businesses to repay debt. Although consumer credit card balances have reduced during the pandemic, the number of people with problem debt remains high.[46] Why? There seem to be two causes. Poverty-stricken households borrow larger numbers of high-interest but smaller value loans. Some of those households have rising rent arrears, heralding a new social problem.

Reduced trade with Europe and inadequate new opportunities will bring reduced incomes to the population. This is today's social problem, not one that can wait fifteen years for a solution. The proportion of economic output to be wasted on paying interest will rise as the economy shrinks.[47] Brexit will drive the United Kingdom closer to its financial system limit. Perhaps the United Kingdom will become a new case study in lieu of Puerto Rico.

The challenge to be faced by the combination of Britain's real debt problem, Brexit and the financial system limit, is unrecognised.

REFERENCES

1. This book uses the generic term coronavirus rather than the specific virus name Covid-19 because it is widely recognised by the public.

2. https://www.theglobaleconomy.com/rankings/household_debt_gdp/ accessed 3 November 2019.

3. https://www.ons.gov.uk/economy/grossdomesticproduct gdp/timeseries/ihyp/pn2 accessed 17 June 2020, Open Government Licence v. 3.0

4. Three month Treasury Bill chart courtesy of The Chartstore (www.thechartstore.com). Average cost of US consumer credit bearing finance charges taken from wallethub.com, accessed 6 December 2019. As some e-readers do not display large diagrams effectively, Figures 1 and 7 are available to view at www.sparklingbooks.com/limit.html

5. Bloomberg website and Credit Suisse wealth report accessed 9 May 2019. See https://www.bloomberg.com/news/articles/2019-01-15/global-debt-of-244-trillion-nears-record-despite-faster-growth and https://www.credit-suisse.com/media/

assets/corporate/docs/about-us/research/publications/global-wealth-report-2018-en.pdf

6. *Financial Times,* 19 June 2019, *Transparency can stop countries falling deeper into debt.*

7. KPMG cost of capital study 2018: see https://assets.kpmg/content/dam/kpmg/ch/pdf/cost-of-capital-study-2018.pdf, accessed 7 November 2019.

8. Data taken from https://www.robeco.com/ch/en/insights/2018/09/bond-corporate-bond.html accessed 7 November 2019.

9. UK interest rate statistics are confusing. The Bank of England publish rates that they collect from a sample of 24 large banks, based on major lines of business only, for the purpose of estimating the sensitivity of the United Kingdom economy to interest rate changes. The data collection exercise excludes well over 300 medium and smaller monetary financial institutions. Normally the best borrowing rates for the least risky propositions can be obtained from large banks and therefore the sample will not provide an accurate average interest rate. The published interest rate calculation also excludes credit card fees (*source:* enquiry to the Bank of England). In my view, it is not possible to take this data and use it as any basis for calculating true interest costs for all borrowers. The UK mortgage market is dominated by fixed-term deals. At the end of the term, the borrower either takes a pre-set default rate or shops around. One effect of the pandemic will be to make it difficult for many borrowers to move their borrowing elsewhere and therefore pre-set default rates will matter more in the future. These are typically 2% to 3% above fixed rates.

It is even harder to reconcile the various data sources reported. For example, the official (Bankstats) tables for May 2020 (updated 7th July 2020) show individual overdrafts costing 15.20% for a combination of interest and fees, but also report overdraft rates of 31.53% in a different table. Other differences arise with personal loans and credit cards. These factors suggest there may be unmeasured costs of credit. The official data is no doubt as perfect as is practical for its intended purpose but is not suitable for accurate calculation of the true interest spend by individuals and households.

10. March 2020 credit card interest cost courtesy of The Money Charity, https://themoneycharity.org.uk/money-stats-march-2020-portrait-pre-crisis-uk/ accessed 28 April 2020 (Copyright The Money Charity 2020).

11. https://tradingeconomics.com/bonds, accessed 2 July 2019.

12. https://www.ons.gov.uk/economy/grossdomesticproductgdp and https://www.ons.gov.uk/economy/inflationand priceindices both accessed 30 April 2020, Open Government Licence v. 3.0.

13. Strictly these should be compound percentage changes, but when numbers are small, simple arithmetic has almost the same numerical effect. The difference is not material.

14. https://www.mof.go.jp/english/jgbs/publication/newsletter/jgb2019_06e.pdf and https://www.mof.go.jp/english/jgbs/reference/gbb/index.htm both accessed 29 April 2020, Government of Japan Standard Terms and Use (Version 2.0), *Financial Times* 14 October 2019 *Foreign investors have 'kept the faith' in UK government debt* and https://en.wikipedia.org/wiki/National_debt_of_the_United_States accessed 30 April 2020.

15. https://data.worldbank.org/indicator/fb.ast.nper.zs accessed 3 November 2019.

16. *The Economist*, 2 May 2019, *The past decade has brought a compliance boom in banking*. See also *Financial Times*, FTfm, 13 January 2020, *Basel derivative rules point to more pain*.

17. Modern Monetary Theory originated with the economist/engineer Warren B Mosler and is now championed by Prof. Stephanie Kelton of Stony Brook University. The statements about the natural rate of interest being zero and that debt can expand 'without limit' are taken from a lecture given by Prof. Kelton in Zurich on 21 January 2020. The 'without limit' claim originated with Dr Alan Greenspan.

18. Thomas Piketty, *Capital in the Twenty-First Century*, Harvard University Press 2014, translated by Arthur Goldhammer.

19. *The Economist*, 12 October 2019, *The world economy's strange new rules*.

20. *Financial Times*, 16 October 2019, *We are playing with fire in a wooden home*.

21. *Financial Times*, Letters, 29 October 2019, *Negative rates and the Swedish experience*. See also *Financial Times*, Big Read, 21 February 2020.

22. See *Bloomberg News*, 4 October 2019, *Memorandum on ECB Monetary Policy* by Issing, Stark, Schlesinger and also *Financial Times*, 7 October 2019, *The Euro's Guardians face a roar of the dinosaur*.

23. https://www.cnbc.com/2019/06/16/puerto-ricos-oversight-board-strikes-35-billion-restructuring-deal-with-common wealths-bondholders.html, accessed 5 August 2019. In order to estimate debt interest cost in relation to GDP, the calculation

here assumes pension debt is also repayable over thirty years.

24. https://www.gao.gov/assets/700/691675.pdf accessed 17 June 2020.

25. http://www.cadtm.org/Who-Owns-Puerto-Rico-s-Debt-Exactly-We-ve-Tracked-Down-10-of-the-Biggest, accessed 5 August 2019.

26. *Jubilee Debt Campaign*, 9 January 2020, *The increasing global South debt crisis and cuts in public spending* https://jubileedebt.org.uk/report/the-increasing-global-south-debt-crisis-and-cuts-in-public-spending, accessed 12 January 2020.

27. *Financial Times*, 17 January 2018, *Carillion held just £29m in cash when it collapsed.*

28. https://www.fnlondon.com/articles/jpmorgan-and-ubs-take-a-hit-on-carillion-debt-20180117

29. https://www.constructionnews.co.uk/news/contractors-news/carillion-construction-had-6-9bn-liabilities-when-it-collapsed-14-04-2018/

30. *The Guardian*, 29 August 2017, *Pension deficit of UK's leading companies equivalent to 70% of their profits.* Guardian News & Media Ltd open licence.

31. https://www.ppf.co.uk/ppf-7800-index accessed 17 June 2020.

32. Adair Turner, *Between Debt and the Devil*, Princeton University Press, 2015. The notable exceptions to a government monopoly on issuing banknotes are Scotland and Northern Ireland, although the notes issued by commercial banks are fully backed by the Bank of England.

33. Keynes also proposed a recycling mechanism for global surpluses. In *The Global Minotaur* (Zed Books, 2015) Yanis Varoufakis describes post-war global cash flows and suggests that surplus recycling has now ceased – perhaps it has been blocked by the financial system limit.

34. https://www.imf.org/en/About/Factsheets/Sheets/2016/08/01/14/51/Special-Drawing-Right-SDR accessed 25 May 2020.

35. For example, see Walter Scheidel, *The Great Leveler,* Princeton University Press 2017.

36. Nigel Lawson, when Chancellor of the Exchequer in 1986, forced defined benefit pension schemes with surpluses of over 5% to either improve pension benefits or take a break from paying contributions. If they did neither then they would have to refund the surplus to the sponsoring company which in turn would pay 40% tax on the refund. Most schemes chose to take a contribution holiday. Until 1997, pension schemes could reclaim 10% tax on dividend income, but the tax credit was abolished by Gordon Brown, at an estimated cost of £10 bn p.a.

37. *The Observer,* 17 December 2017, *Why business could prosper under a Corbyn government.*

38. *Financial Times,* 27 April 2010, *Basel rules must address shortfalls of the past.*

39. *The Economist,* 18 May 2019, *Consolidation programme.*

40. The UK's decisive decade, Resolution Foundation May 2021, *https://economy2030.resolutionfoundation.org/wp-content/uploads/2021/04/The-UKs-decisive-decade.pdf* accessed 18 May 2021.

41. Page 13 of the report refers to "debt levels at over 100% of

GDP" without noting that the 100% figure more properly refers only to *government* debt. Private sector debt is unquantified.

42. Aston University have calculated that Brexit caused a cumulative loss of service sales to the EU-27 of £113 bn between 2016 and 2019, *before* the United Kingdom left the EU, with Ireland the greatest beneficiary. See *https://www.aston. ac.uk/latest-news/irish-eyes-smiling-brexit-sees-services-trade-switch-uk-new-research* accessed 1 June 2021.

43. For an example, consider this headline from the Sunday Express 23 May 2021: "'Stars have aligned!' £8 bn Brexit trade bonanza looms as UK set sights on South Africa" (see *https:// www.express.co.uk/news/politics/1439540/brexit-news-uk-trade-south-africa-latest-andrew-selous* accessed 26 May 2021). The £8 bn bonanza referred to is the actual value of existing UK trade with South Africa as shown on the *gov. uk* website. This can be understood by reading the article carefully, checking *https://www.gov.uk/guidance/uk-trade-agreements-with-non-eu-countries* and following the links given on that page.

44. Arrangements for visa-free work are always reciprocal. The EU offered its usual 90 day permission and required 90 day access for EU nationals in return. The Home Office insisted that entertainment professionals from anywhere in the world only should work in the UK for 30 days visa-free. The EU cannot be expected to change its border procedures for one profession in one country out of over 160 non-members; UK musicians therefore have no right to work except on individual country rules.

45. Many small and under-developed countries, particularly in the Pacific region, have cooperation agreements with the EU

rather than free trade agreements. A number of countries, including those in the Gulf Cooperation Council, are negotiating trade agreements with both the EU and UK. Sanctioned countries such as Belarus, Iran, North Korea and Venezuela, have no trade agreements with either the EU or UK. It is impossible for all these countries to replace Britain's damaged European trade, particularly in services which have to be delivered in nearby countries with equivalent standards.

46. See *https://themoneycharity.org.uk/money-stats-may-2021-wider-economic-recovery-tempered-significant-proportion-households-financial-distress/* accessed 23 June 2021 (Copyright The Money Charity 2021).

47. See also "The contrast between inflation and deflation" in chapter 10.

INDEX

The notations pp*f* and pp*t* refer to a figure or table on the stated page.
The notation pp*n*xx refers to note xx on the stated page.

150

Sparkling Books

We publish:

- Crime
- Mystery
- Thriller
- Suspense

- Horror
- Romance
- YA fiction
- Non-fiction

All titles are available as e-books
from your e-book retailer.

For current list of titles visit:

www.sparklingbooks.com

@SparklingBooks